EMPLOYEE BENEFITS PRACTICE FROM WILEY LAW PUBLICATIONS

EMPLOYEE BENEFITS: VALUATION, ANALYSIS, AND STRATEGIES
Steven G. Vernon, The Wyatt Company

EMPLOYER'S GUIDE TO SOCIAL SECURITY
Robert Heitzman, Jr.

FAMILY AND MEDICAL LEAVE: POLICIES AND PROCEDURES
Richard L. Marcus

FEDERAL REGULATION OF EMPLOYEE BENEFITS
James O. Castagnera and David A. Littell

401(K) PLANS: A COMPREHENSIVE GUIDE
Bruce J. McNeil and Michael E. Lloyd

FUNDAMENTALS OF FLEXIBLE COMPENSATION (SECOND EDITION)
Karen L. Frost, Dale L. Gifford, Christine A. Seltz, and Kenneth L. Sperling—Hewitt Associates

MANAGING COBRA: THE COMPLETE COMPLIANCE GUIDE
Ari Cowan and Lee T. Paterson

MANAGING HEALTH CARE FOR THE ELDERLY
Cynthia Polich, Marcie Parker, Margaret Hottinger, and Deborah Chase

MANAGING WORKERS' COMPENSATION: A HUMAN RESOURCES GUIDE TO CONTROLLING COSTS
Janet R. Douglas

PENSION PLAN TERMINATIONS
Thomas Veal and Edward R. Mackiewicz

RETIREMENT SAVINGS PLANS: DESIGN, REGULATION & ADMINISTRATION OF CASH OR DEFERRED ARRANGEMENTS
David A. Littell, Donald C. Cardamone, and Wilhelm L. Gruszecki

FAMILY AND MEDICAL LEAVE
POLICIES AND PROCEDURES

SUBSCRIPTION NOTICE

This Wiley product is updated on a periodic basis with supplements to reflect important changes in the subject matter. If you purchased this product directly from John Wiley & Sons, Inc., we have already recorded your subscription for this update service.

If, however, you purchased this product from a bookstore and wish to receive (1) the current update at no additional charge, and (2) future updates and revised or related volumes billed separately with a 30-day examination review, please send your name, company name (if applicable), address and the title of the product to:

Supplement Department
John Wiley & Sons, Inc.
One Wiley Drive
Somerset, NJ 08875
1-800-225-5945

For customers outside the United States, please contact the Wiley office nearest you:

Professional and Reference Division
John Wiley & Sons Canada, Ltd.
22 Worcester Road
Rexdale, Ontario M9W 1L1
CANADA
(416) 236-3580
Phone: 1-800-263-1590
Fax: 1-800-675-6599

John Wiley & Sons, Ltd.
Baffins Lane
Chichester
West Sussex, PO19 1UD
UNITED KINGDOM
Phone: (44) (243) 779777

Jacaranda Wiley Ltd.
PRT Division
P.O. Box 174
North Ryde, NSW 2113
AUSTRALIA
Phone: (02) 805-1100
Fax: (02) 805-1597

John Wiley & Sons (SEA) Pte. Ltd.
37 Jalan Pemimpin
Block B # 05-04
Union Industrial Building
SINGAPORE 2057
Phone: (65) 258-1157

FAMILY AND MEDICAL LEAVE POLICIES AND PROCEDURES

RICHARD L. MARCUS

Sonnenschein, Nath & Rosenthal
Chicago, Illinois

Wiley Law Publications
JOHN WILEY & SONS, INC.
New York • Chichester • Brisbane • Toronto • Singapore

This text is printed on acid-free paper.

Library of Congress Cataloging-in-Publication Data

ISBN 0-471-04195-5

Printed in the United States of America

10 9 8 7 6 5 4 3 2 1

PREFACE

Although several earlier versions of proposed federal family and medical leave laws encountered substantial opposition in Congress and the Executive Branch, the Family and Medical Leave Act of 1993 (FMLA) passed the House and Senate with relative ease and was quickly signed into law by President Clinton on February 5, 1993. It went into effect six months later, on August 5.

At the time FMLA was enacted, the United States General Accounting Office predicted that, each year, approximately 2.5 million workers would take leaves of absence under its terms—at an annual estimated price to employers (representing only the cost of maintaining health insurance for workers out on leave) of $674 million. As this is written, it is of course far too early to tell whether the GAO's prediction and estimate are realistic. It is likewise too early and, in any event, unlikely we will ever really know the extent to which FMLA may be misused to mask chronic absenteeism and preserve the jobs of its practitioners.

This book is intended to analyze FMLA, point out to employers some of its obvious and not so obvious practical ramifications, and offer them suggestions for some practical ways to deal with it. As is typical of social legislation like FMLA, the statute itself is relatively brief and broadly worded. It was left to the Department of Labor to develop the specifics, and on June 4, 1993, the DOL issued interim regulations which filled forty-five pages of the Federal Register. These interim regulations, and the statute itself, are discussed and analyzed in substantial detail.

FMLA deals, in part at least, with employees and their family members who suffer serious health conditions. Both the legislative history of FMLA and the interim regulations show that Congress and the Department of Labor were aware of the close relationship and potential overlap between FMLA and other existing legislation dealing with such matters, particularly the Americans With Disabilities Act of 1990 (ADA). I have tried to focus on that relationship and its practical ramifications. Attention is also devoted to specific issues likely to confront the employer whose employees are covered by collective bargaining agreements.

Chapter 7 contains the full text of FMLA and the Department of Labor's interim regulations.

Chicago, Illinois
February 1994

RICHARD L. MARCUS

HOW TO USE THIS BOOK

General

This manual provides an up-to-date overview and summary of the requirements of the Family and Medical Leave Act of 1993 (FMLA). The FMLA, which was enacted on February 5, 1993, entitles qualified employees to as much as 12 weeks of unpaid leave under certain circumstances. The major provisions of the FMLA and the interim regulations implementing it are outlined below. Citations are to Sections contained in Titles I and IV of Public Law 103–3, 29 U.S.C. 2601 et. seq., cited as "FMLA § __" and Interim Final Regulations Issued by Department of Labor, which became effective on August 5, 1993, 29 CFR Part 825, cited as "Regs. § __")

[WARN] *This reference does not provide binding legal, policy design, or legislative information. Since the legal, policy design, and legislative environments are constantly changing, employers should seek the advice of qualified professionals, where and when appropriate.*

Organization

This reference is organized into 7 chapters, described in the following sections.

Chapter 1: COVERAGE. Refer to this unit for a detailed description of the employers and employees covered by FMLA.

Chapter 2: LEAVE PROVISIONS. Refer to this unit for information about FMLA's leave provisions, including reasons for which leave can be taken.

Chapter 3: BENEFITS PROTECTED. Refer to this unit for an explanation of the benefits FMLA protects. It includes a discussion of reasons why employers may, in certain cases, deny job restoration to employees returning to work from a FMLA leave.

Chapter 4: OTHER OBLIGATIONS OF THE EMPLOYER. Refer to this unit for information regarding the employer's record-keeping and posting requirements.

Chapter 5: PROHIBITED CONDUCT, ENFORCEMENT PROCEDURES, AND REMEDIES. Refer to this unit for a detailed discussion of the employer's prohibited conduct, as well as the enforcement procedures and remedies available to employees and the Secretary of Labor.

Chapter 6: MISCELLANEOUS PROVISIONS. Refer to this unit for an overview of the effective date of FMLA, as well as how FMLA affects other state and federal laws.

Chapter 7: STATUTE AND REGULATIONS. Refer to this unit for the text of FMLA and the Interim Final Regulations issued by the Department of Labor.

APPENDIXES. Refer to this unit for reference material pertaining to the FMLA.

ABOUT THE AUTHOR

Richard L. Marcus is the head of the Labor and Employment Practice Group at the firm of Sonnenschein Nath and Rosenthal. He is a graduate of the University of Chicago Law School where he served as a member of the Editorial Board of the University of Chicago Law Review. He has been a member of the Visiting Committees of the Law School and the University's Division of Humanities. Throughout his professional career Mr. Marcus has represented management in all areas relating to labor and employment law, including collective bargaining and matters arising under the entire gamut of federal labor and employment laws, including the National Labor Relations Act, Fair Labor Standards Act, Occupational Safety & Health Act, Worker Adjustment & Retraining Notification Act, Equal Employment Opportunities Act, Age Discrimination in Employment Act, and the Americans with Disabilities Act, as well as a variety of related state laws. Mr. Marcus has represented employers in proceedings at all levels in state and federal courts and administrative agencies, including the National Labor Relations Board, the Department of Labor, the Equal Employment Opportunity Commission, and the Office of Federal Contract Compliance. He is a nationally recognized speaker; regularly addresses employer groups and associations throughout the United States; and has participated in numerous seminars sponsored by government agencies, universities, and trade associations. Mr. Marcus is a member of the Labor & Employment Law Section of the American Bar Association and has been a member of the Section's Committee on Practice and Procedure before the National Labor Relations Board as well as its Committee on Federal Labor Standards Legislation. His name has been included in all published editions of "The Best Lawyers in America."

SUMMARY CONTENTS

DETAILED CONTENTS

SHORT REFERENCE LIST

The following is a listing of abbreviations used throughout this workbook.

Short Reference	*Full Reference*
ADA	Americans With Disabilities Act
COBRA	Consolidated Omnibus Budget Reconciliation Act of 1986
DOL	Department of Labor
ERISA	Employee Retirement Income Security Act
FLSA	Fair Labor Standards Act
FMLA	Family and Medical Leave Act of 1993
WARN	Worker Adjustment and Retraining Notification Act

Special Symbols

This reference is designed for "hands-on" use. You will find key areas are highlighted in the margin by the following graphic symbols.

Symbol	*Definition*
[FED]	Denotes important federal legislation.
[REGS]	Denotes important federal regulation.
[STATE]	Denotes important state legislation or regulation.
[!]	Denotes an important point to consider.
[WARN]	WARNING notation: Review carefully before proceeding.
[**]	Denotes a hint or a useful idea.

CHAPTER 1

COVERAGE

§ 1.1 Overview

[FED]

On February 5, 1993, the Family and Medical Leave Act of 1993 (FMLA) was signed into law.[1] Under the FMLA, employees who qualify may be entitled to as much as 12 weeks of unpaid leave under certain circumstances. The FMLA confers a number of new rights on qualified employees and creates a host of new obligations for covered employers. As a result, employers will be confronted with issues which will significantly impact many of their employment practices.

Generally, the effective date of the FMLA is August 5, 1993. The exception to this date is that for employees covered by collective bargaining

[1] Public Law 103-3, 29 U.S.C. §§ 2601 *et seq.*

agreements in effect on August 5, 1993, the effective date of the FMLA is the termination date of the agreement or February 5, 1994, whichever is first.[2]

[REGS]

On June 3, 1993, interim rules governing FMLA were issued by the Labor Department.[3] These rules are set out fully in **Chapter 7**.

§ 1.2 Covered Employers

The FMLA applies to:

- Any business entity or individual (corporations, partnerships, and so forth)
- engaged in commerce or in an any industry affecting commerce
- who employs 50 or more employees
- for each working day during 20 or more calendar weeks (which need not be consecutive) during the current or preceding calendar year.[4]

[!] But, even though an employer is covered, some or even all of its employees might still not be eligible for any benefits under FMLA. (See **§ 1.9**.)

§ 1.3 —Who Is Employed

The interim final regulations issued by the Department of Labor (DOL)[5] use a "maintained on the payroll" test to determine whether an employee is employed for each working day of the workweek.

Under the "maintained on the payroll" test:

- An employee who is on the employer's payroll for each day of the workweek is counted.

---

[2] FMLA § 405. References herein are to Sections contained in Titles I and IV of Public Law 103-3, §§ 29 U.S.C. 2601 *et seq.* cited as "FMLA § ____."

[3] Interim Regulations Issued by the Department of Labor on June 3, 1993, 29 CFR Part 825, cited as "Regs. § ____."

[4] FMLA § 101(4).

[5] *See* **Ch. 7**.

- It is not necessary that an employee actually work on each day of the workweek or that the employee receive compensation for the week.[6]
- Conversely, an employee hired in the middle of the workweek or terminated before the end of the workweek would not be employed for each day of *that* workweek, and therefore would not be counted under the FMLA for that workweek.[7]

Leave/Layoff

Under the "maintained on the payroll" test, employees out on leave are counted as long as the employer has a reasonable expectation that the employee will later return to active employment. On the other hand, employees on layoff (whether temporary, indefinite, or long-term) are not counted.[8]

§ 1.4 —Integrated Employers

Separate corporate entities are deemed to be a single employer if they are "integrated." Four factors are considered (no one of which is determinative) to decide if related employers are integrated:

- Common management
- Interrelation of operations
- Centralized control of labor relations
- Degree of common ownership or financial control

If employers are deemed integrated, then all employees of the integrated employers must be counted in determining employer coverage.[9]

§ 1.5 —Joint Employers

For purposes of determining whether an employer has a sufficient number of employees to be a covered employer, employees "jointly employed" by

---

[6] Thus, part-time employees, like full-time employees, are considered to be employed each working day of the calendar week, as long as they are maintained on the payroll.

[7] Regs. § 825.105.

[8] Regs. § 825.105.

[9] Moreover, if employers are deemed integrated, then all employees of the integrated employers must be counted in determining employee eligibility as well. *See* **§ 1.9**.

two employers must be counted by *both* employers even if they are maintained on only one of the employers' payrolls.

[!] "Leased" employees and employees supplied through agencies *are* included in the total count of employees for purposes of determining whether the employer is covered by FMLA.

Joint Employers: Factors

The factors normally considered in determining whether an employment relationship exists for purposes of the joint employment test are:

1. nature and degree of control of the worker
2. degree of supervision
3. power to determine rate and method of payment
4. authority to hire, fire, or modify conditions of employment
5. preparation of the payroll and payment of wages

No single factor is conclusive.

Example
An employee is jointly employed where two employers agree to share the employee's services or to use the employee interchangeably.

Primary and Secondary Employers

The FMLA distinguishes between "primary" and "secondary" employers. Only primary employers must fully comply with all of the obligations under the FMLA, including giving of required notices, providing the leave, maintaining benefits during leaves, and job restoration. The obligations of secondary employers regarding "joint" employees are limited to not committing a "prohibited act" as defined by the FMLA (for example, not discriminating or retaliating against an employee for exercising rights under the FMLA).[10] Note, however, that secondary employers must comply fully with the FMLA regarding their own regular, permanent workforce—even if, standing alone, that workforce consists of less than the requisite number of employees. [**]

Primary Employer: Factors

Factors considered in determining whether an employer is the primary employer include:

---

[10] *See* Ch. 5.

- The authority to hire, fire, and assign work
- Provision of benefits
- Maintenance on the payroll

§ 1.6 —Successors in Interest

A "successor in interest" is one employer who follows another employer in ownership or control of the employing entity. If an employer is found to be the successor in interest to an employer who was covered by the FMLA, an eligible employee's entitlement to leave under the FMLA is the same under the successor employer as it was under the predecessor employer.

Successor in Interest: Factors

As with the tests for integrated and joint employers, a number of factors are considered in determining whether an employer is a successor in interest, no one of which is determinative.[11] The factors include:

- Substantial continuity of operations and workforce
- Use of the same facility
- Similarity of jobs, working conditions, supervisory personnel, equipment, products, or services
- The ability of the predecessor to provide relief to an employee whose rights are violated (during employment with the predecessor)

§ 1.7 —Persons Acting in the Interest of the Employer

Included in the definition of "employer" are individuals acting directly or indirectly in the interest of an employer to any employee. Individuals acting in the interest of an employer (such as corporate officers) are individually liable for violations of the FMLA.

§ 1.8 —Period of Coverage

Once an employer meets the 50-employee/20-week threshold, it will remain covered by the FMLA until it reaches a point where it no longer

---

[11] Regs. § 825.107.

employs 50 employees for 20 weeks during the current and preceding calendar years.

Example

An employer has 60 employees for over 20 weeks prior to August 5, 1993. Thus, the employer meets the test on August 5, 1993. Later during 1993, the employer's work force drops to 45 employees where it remains throughout 1994. Even though the employer no longer meets the test, the employer will still be covered for the remainder of 1993 and for all of 1994.

§ 1.9 Eligible Employees

An employee is eligible for family and medical leave if he or she is all of the following:

- Employed by a covered employer for a minimum of 12 months
- Has worked at least 1,250 hours during the 12 months prior to the commencement of the leave
- Is employed at a worksite at which the employer employs 50 or more employees, including employees employed within 75 miles of the affected employee's worksite[12]

§ 1.10 —Employee Eligibility Distinguished from Covered Employer

Although part-time and temporary employees are counted for purposes of determining whether an employer is covered by the FMLA, such employees are not eligible for leave under the FMLA unless they satisfy all of the required criteria.

§ 1.11 —Hours Worked

In determining the number of hours an employee has worked, the FMLA uses the same test used under the Fair Labor Standards Act (FLSA). Under that test, all hours an employer suffers or permits an employee to work are counted toward the 1,250 threshold.[13] Also, under this test, it is possible

[12] FMLA § 101(2).

[13] *See* 29 CFR Part 785.

for an employee to accumulate "hours of work" without actually performing work. Examples include on-call time or ground time for flight crews.[14]

§ 1.12 —Hours-Months Worked: Date of Determination

The determination of whether the employee has worked at least 1,250 hours in the last 12 months and has been employed for a total of at least 12 months (which need not be consecutive[15]) must be made as of the date the leave begins.

[**] If an employee notifies the employer of the need for a leave before the employee meets the eligibility requirements, the employer may project whether the employee will meet the requirements as of the date of the leave, or the employer may advise the employee when he or she has satisfied the requirements. If the employer confirms an employee's eligibility by using a projection, the employer cannot later challenge the employee's eligibility.

Exempt Employees

In the event no records are kept for employees who are classified as exempt under the Fair Labor Standards Act, it is presumed that such employee has worked at least 1,250 hours, if he or she has worked at least 12 months for the employer.[16]

§ 1.13 —75-Mile Limitation

In order to be eligible, the employee must be employed at a worksite at which the employer employs 50 or more employees. This number includes employees which are employed within 75 miles from the relevant worksite, based on surface miles on public roads.[17]

---

[14] Regs. § 825.110.

[15] Regs. § 825.110.

[16] Regs. § 825.110.

[17] Regs. § 825.111. The interim regulations adopt the "single site of employment" test contained in the Worker Adjustment and Retraining Notification Act (WARN) for determining what constitutes a "worksite" under the FMLA.

Example

An employer has 2 facilities which are more than 75 miles apart (measured by road miles over public roads and waterways). Facility A has 100 employees and Facility B has 45 employees. Only the employees at Facility A may be eligible for leave under the FMLA.

Employees Without a Fixed Worksite

For employees without a fixed worksite (for example, construction workers), the worksite is one of the following:

- The site assigned as home base
- The site from which the work is assigned
- The site to which the employee reports

§ 1.14 —Number of Employees: Date of Determination

The determination of whether an employer has 50 employees within a 75-mile radius is to be made at the time the employee requests the leave. If an employer does not have the requisite number of employees at that time, the employee may renew his or her leave request at a later time.

[!] Once an employee is determined eligible after requesting a leave, that eligibility will not be affected by any subsequent change in the number of employees employed at or within 75 miles of the worksite.

Example

In August, an employee who is one of 60 employees working at a single worksite requests a FMLA leave to begin in December. The employer must grant the leave even though it knows that the workforce will be less than 50 in December and even though the workforce does, in fact, shrink below 50.

CHAPTER 2

LEAVE PROVISIONS

§ 2.1 Entitlement to Leave

An eligible employee is entitled to up to 12 weeks of leave during any 12-month period for one or more of the reasons set forth in FMLA. ***The leave need not be paid.***

§ 2.2 —Calculation of "Weeks" of Leave

Only the amount of leave actually taken can be counted against the 12 weeks to which the employee is entitled, and the number of "weeks" allowed or taken must be determined with reference to the employee's normal work schedule. This calculation may require conversion of hourly or daily schedules to weekly equivalents, particularly in the case of intermittent or reduced schedule leaves.

Example
An employee who normally works 30 hours per week whose schedule is reduced to 20 hours as a result of FMLA leave will be taking 1/3 of a week's leave each week.

Example
An employee whose normal 5-day per week schedule is reduced to 4 days as a result of FMLA leave will be taking 1/5 of a week's leave each week.

Where the employee's work schedule varies from week to week, an average based upon the 12 weeks immediately preceding the FMLA leave period will be used to determine the employee's "normal" schedule.[1]

§ 2.3 Time Period Within Which Leave May Be Taken

The employer may choose one of four methods for measuring the 12-month period as long as the method chosen is applied consistently and uniformly. The choices are:

- The calendar year
- A fixed year based on some other measure, such as a fiscal year or a year starting from an anniversary date
- A 12-month period measured forward from the first date leave is used
- A "rolling" 12-month period measured backward from the date leave is used.[2]

Prevention of "Stacking." The fourth alternative is most likely to prevent employees from "stacking" leave from one year to the next.

---

[1] Regs. § 825.205.

[2] Regs. § 825.200. Note that no leave taken prior to the effective date of FMLA can be charged against the amount of FMLA leave available to the employee.

Notice of Change in Method of Calculation. An employer who wishes to change the method of calculating the 12-month period in which leave can be used must give employees 60 days' notice and must not use the change in method to avoid its obligations under FMLA.

§ 2.4 Overview of Reasons for Which Leave Can Be Taken

An eligible employee is entitled to leave for one or more of the following four reasons:[3]

1. **Birth.** The birth of a son or daughter of an employee, in order to care for the son or daughter
2. **Adoption or Foster Care.** The placement of a son or daughter with the employee for adoption or foster care
3. **Serious Health Condition of Family Member.** To care for a spouse, son, daughter, or parent who has a "serious health condition"
4. **Serious Health Condition of Employee.** If a "serious health condition" renders the employee unable to perform the functions of his or her job

§ 2.5 Leave for Birth, Adoption, or Foster Care

FMLA contains the following provisions applicable to leave taken for the birth, or placement for adoption or foster care of a son or daughter:

Adoption/Foster Care. In order to qualify for leave based upon the placement of a child for adoption, it is not necessary that the adoption be accomplished through a state-licensed adoption agency. With respect to foster care (which is 24-hour care for another's child), however, the interim regulations require action by the state (for example, a court determination), and an informal arrangement to care for another person's child does not qualify.[4]

---

[3] FMLA § 102(a)(1)(A)-(D).

[4] Regs. § 825.112(e).

[**] In the case of birth, leave is available only if it is necessary to enable the employee to "care for" the child. There is no such "care for" requirement with respect to adoption or foster care placement. Note also that, for purposes of determining the employee's entitlement to leave, there is no maximum age limit on the child being adopted or placed for foster care.[5]

Timing of Leave. Leave occasioned by a child's birth, or placement for adoption or foster care must be completed within 12 months following the birth or the placement of the child. The leave may begin before the actual adoption or foster home placement of the child, where the employee's absence is required in order to allow the adoption or placement proceedings to proceed (for example, to attend counseling sessions, court appearances, conferences with attorneys, doctors and agency personnel, or physical examinations).[6]

Gender-Neutral. These leave provisions are gender-neutral, applying equally to both male and female employees.[7]

Spouses Working for Same Employer. If a husband and wife work for the same employer, they are only entitled to an *aggregate* leave of 12 weeks from that employer during any 12 month period in order to care for a newborn child or a child placed for adoption or foster care. This is true even if the spouses work at different sites or in different divisions maintained by their common employer.

[!] While an employer may insist that his employee-spouses aggregate their leaves, decisions as to how (or if) the aggregate leave is to be shared cannot be imposed by the employer.

§ 2.6 Leave Based on the Serious Health Condition of a Family Member

With respect to leaves taken as the result of a serious health condition of a son, daughter, spouse, or parent of an employee, FMLA provides as follows:

Definition of Son, Daughter, Spouse, and Parent. The terms *son* and *daughter* mean a child under the age of 18, including "biological, adopted,

---

[5] Regs. § 825.112(d).

[6] Regs. §§ 825.201, 825.112.

[7] Regs. § 825.112(b).

or foster child, a step child, legal ward, or a child of a person standing in loco parentis." They also include children 18 years of age and older who are "incapable of self-care" because of a physical or mental disability.[8] These definitions are intended to ensure that an employee who actually has the day-to-day responsibility of caring for a child is entitled to leave even if the employee does not have a biological or legal relationship to the child.

FMLA defines *spouse* as "a husband or wife, as the case may be." Under the interim regulations, the determination of whether a person is a spouse is to be made in accordance with applicable state law and, where recognized by the state, it includes common law marriages. However, according to the explanatory provisions published by the Department of Labor with the interim regulations, the term *spouse* does not include unmarried domestic partners.

Parent includes the employee's biological parent as well as one who stands "or stood in loco parentis to [the] employee when the employee was a child." The interim regulations make it clear that the status is not dependent on a biological or legal relationship, and that it does not include a parent in-law.[9]

§ 2.7 FMLA Definition of Serious Health Condition

Under FMLA, a *serious health condition* is defined as "an illness, injury, impairment, or physical or mental condition that involves inpatient care in a hospital, hospice, or residential medical care facility; or continuing treatment by a health care provider."[10]

---

[8] FMLA § 101(12). According to the Regulations, one is "incapable of self-care" if he or she requires active assistance or supervision to provide daily self-care "in several of the 'activities of daily living' " such as "grooming and hygiene, bathing, dressing, eating, cooking, cleaning, shopping, taking public transportaion, paying bills, maintaining a residence, using telephones and directories, using a post office, etc." Regs. § 825.113(c)(1). The Regulations adopt the definitions of Physical or Mental Disability incorporated in the EEOC's regulations applicable to the ADA. 29 CFR part 1630.

[9] Regs. § 825.113.

[10] FMLA § 101(11).

§ 2.8 Regulation Definition of Serious Health Condition

The interim regulations elaborate upon and significantly expand the definition contained in FMLA. Under the regulations, a serious health condition is defined as any injury, illness, impairment, or physical or mental condition which involves either:

- ***Inpatient Care.*** Any period of incapacity or treatment in connection with, or consequent to, inpatient care (meaning an overnight stay) in a hospital, hospice, or residential medical care facility
- ***Absence for 3 Calendar Days.*** Any period of incapacity requiring absence from work, school, or other "regular daily activities," of more than three calendar days, which also involves "continuing treatment" by, or under the supervision of, a "health care provider"
- ***Continuing Treatment.*** Continuing treatment by, or under the supervision of, a health care provider of a chronic or long-term health condition that is incurable or "so serious that, if not treated, would likely result in a period of incapacity of more than three calendar days"; or continuing treatment for prenatal care[11]

Health Care Provider. The term *health care provider* includes:

- Doctors of medicine and osteopathy
- Podiatrists, dentists, clinical psychologists, optometrists, and chiropractors (but only where treatment involves manual manipulation of the spine to correct a partial dislocation shown to exist by an x-ray) authorized to practice in the state
- Nurse practitioners and nurse mid-wives authorized to practice under state law
- Christian Science practitioners[12]

Continuing Treatment. The interim regulations indicate that a family member is considered to be under "continuing treatment by a health care provider" if:

- ***Treatments by Health Care Provider.*** The family member is treated *two or more times* for the particular injury or illness either by the health care provider or by a nurse or doctor's assistant under the health care provider's direct supervision.

---

[11] Regs. §§ 825.114, 825.800.

[12] Regs. §§ 825.118, 825.800.

- ***Treatments by Provider of Health Care Services.*** The family member is treated for the particular injury or illness *two or more times* by a provider of health care services such as a physical therapist under the orders of, or on referral by, a health care provider, or is treated *at least once* by a health care provider which results in a continuing regimen of medication, therapy, or other treatment under the supervision of the health care provider to resolve the condition.
- ***Continuing Supervision.*** The family member is under the continuing supervision *but not necessarily the active treatment* of a health care provider due to a serious long-term or chronic condition or disability which cannot be cured, for example Alzheimer's disease, or a severe stroke.[13]

Conditions Not Covered. The term *serious health condition* does not include "routine preventive physical examinations" or voluntary or cosmetic treatments which are not "medically necessary"; *BUT* the interim regulations suggest that if such treatments require inpatient hospital care, they *will* qualify as "serious health conditions."

> [!] "Treatments for allergies or stress, or for substance abuse, are serious health conditions if all the conditions of the regulation are met."[14]

§ 2.9 Employee's Role as Necessary Care Giver

In order for an employee to qualify for leave to care for a seriously ill family member, a health care provider may be required to certify that the "employee is needed to care for" the family member.[15] Such a need may involve "physical and psychological" care, including providing for the family member's medical, hygienic, nutritional, or safety needs; providing transportation to and from doctors; providing psychological comfort and reassurance; and making arrangements for changes in the family member's care.

Scheduling of Treatments. FMLA provides that the employee must make a "reasonable effort" to schedule the family member's medical treatments in such a way as to avoid unduly disrupting the employer's operations, "subject to the approval of the [family member's] health care provider."[16]

---

[13] Regs. §§ 825.114(3)(b), 825.800.

[14] Regs. § 825.114(c).

[15] FMLA § 103(b)(4)(A); Regs. § 825.114(d).

[16] FMLA § 102(e)(2)(A).

§ 2.10 Other Considerations

Spouses Working for Same Employer. Unlike the situation involving care of a newborn child or a child placed via adoption or foster care,[17] a common employer of husband and wife *cannot* insist that they aggregate their leaves to care for a seriously ill child or each other.[18]

§ 2.11 Leave Based on the Employee's Own Serious Health Condition

With respect to leaves necessitated by the employee's serious health condition, FMLA and the interim regulations provide as follows:

Serious Health Condition. The same definitions discussed above[19] with respect to family members apply in determining whether or not the employee has a health condition serious enough to qualify for FMLA leave.

Inability to Perform. The serious health condition must also be of such a nature that it "makes the employee unable to perform the functions of [his or her] position."[20] According to the interim regulations, this means that the employee must be either unable to work at all or be "unable to perform *any of the essential functions* of the employee's position within the meaning of the Americans with Disabilities Act (ADA)."[21]

[**] The interim regulations do not make it clear whether "any" means all or any one of the essential functions. The context suggests the latter.

[!] The Department of Labor has indicated that an employee would be considered temporarily "unable to perform the functions of the position" when he or she is away from work receiving medical treatment. Thus, even if the employee's *condition* does not presently render the employee unable to perform, the need for treatment of that condition might, and the employee may thereby become entitled to FMLA leave.

---

[17] See **§ 2.5 above.**

[18] FMLA § 102(f)(2) does allow the employer to apply the limitation to spouses' leave to care for a seriously ill "parent." But, as the summary to the interim regulations points out, since there is no FMLA leave available to care for a parent-in-law, the situations where this will apply (where husband and wife have the same parent) "are extremely unlikely."

[19] See **§§ 2.7, 2.8.**

[20] FMLA § 102(a)(1)(D).

[21] Regs. § 825.115.

Scheduling of Treatments. FMLA provides that the employee must make a "reasonable effort" to schedule medical treatments in such a way as to avoid unduly disrupting the employer's operations, "subject to the approval of the [employee's] health care provider."[22]

§ 2.12 Intermittent and Reduced Leave Schedule

Unlike leave for the birth or placement of a son or daughter, leave necessitated by a family member's or the employee's own serious health condition may be taken on an intermittent or reduced schedule basis if it is "medically necessary," and if the need can be best accommodated through an intermittent or reduced leave schedule.[23]

Intermittent Leave. *Intermittent* leave is defined as leave taken in separate periods of time due to a single illness or injury, and may include leave ranging from one hour to several weeks in duration. Such leaves might be necessary, for example, to enable the employee to attend or to provide transportation for a seriously ill family member to attend medical appointments, treatments, and therapy sessions. There is no limit on the duration or frequency of intermittent leaves, but the employer may limit intermittent leave increments to the smallest increment (one hour or less) used in its payroll system.[24]

Reduced Leave Schedule. *Reduced schedule leave* is defined as a "leave schedule that reduces the usual number of hours per workweek, or hours per workday, of an employee." Such a leave may be used, for example, by an employee who is recovering from a serious health condition and is not yet ready to resume full-time employment.

[!] Although an employee unable to work a full schedule may *not* be entitled to demand a reduced schedule under ADA (if, for example, such a schedule would impose undue hardship on the employer), he or she *may* be entitled to demand it under FMLA regardless of the consequences to the employer.

---

22 FMLA § 102(e)(2)(A).

23 FMLA § 102(b)(1); Regs. § 825.203.

24 Regs. § 825.203(d).

Medical Necessity. In order to qualify for intermittent or reduced schedule leave, there must be a medical need "as distinguished from voluntary treatments and procedures" which can best be accommodated by such leaves. Employees needing such leaves must attempt to schedule them "so as not to disrupt the employer's operations."[25]

Temporary Transfer Option. If an employee requests intermittent or reduced schedule leave based on the employee's own or a family member's "forseeable . . . planned medical treatment," the employer may require the employee to temporarily transfer to an "available alternative position" for which the employee is qualified. Such an alternative position must, however, have "equivalent pay and benefits," and "better accommodate" the employee's recurring periods of leave than the employee's regular position. The alternative position might represent a modification of an existing job, but there is no requirement that it involve equivalent duties.[26]

[!] The employer's right to compel the employee's acceptance of an alternative position could well be limited or precluded by the Americans with Disabilities Act, state law, or an applicable collective bargaining agreement.[27]

§ 2.13 Notice of Need for Leave

The employee (or a representative designated by the employee) must give the employer at least 30 days' notice of his or her intention to take leave for the foreseeable birth, adoption, or foster care placement of child, or the planned medical treatment of the employee or a seriously ill family member. If, however, the date of birth, placement or medical treatment requires that leave begin in less than 30 days, the employee need give the employer omly as much notice as is "practicable."

---

[25] Regs. § 825.117.

[26] Regs. § 825.204.

[27] Regs. § 825.204(b).

[!] The requirement that an employee give advance notice as a condition of eligibility for FMLA leave is subject to relaxation or waiver where an applicable collective bargaining agreement, state law, or the employer's practices with respect to employees taking other kinds of leaves require less or no advanced notice.[28]

Practicable Notice. Under the interim regulations, *practicable* is defined to mean as soon as both possible and practical, taking into account all of the facts and circumstances of the individual case. If it is not possible to give 30 days' notice, "as soon as practicable" generally will mean at least verbal notification within one or two business days of the date on which the need for leave becomes known to the employee.

Form of Notice. FMLA does not specify what form of notice the employee is required to give. However, the interim regulations provide that the employee may give the employer verbal notice, and that, regardless of its form, the notice need only be sufficient to make the employer aware that the employee needs FMLA-qualifying leave and the anticipated timing and duration of the leave; however, the employee need not mention FMLA. While the employer may require its employees to comply with its customary notice and procedural requirements for requesting unpaid leave (for example, written notice), the employer may *not* delay an employee's request for FMLA leave if the employee provides timely verbal or other notice—even if the employee fails to comply with the employer's customary requirements.

Effect of Employee's Failure to Give Notice. If an employee fails to give the requisite 30 days' advance notice for forseeable leave without any reasonable excuse for the delay, the employer may deny the leave until at least 30 days after the employee gives notice to the employer. The interim regulations make it clear, however, that the employer *cannot* deny or postpone the leave unless *all* of the following conditions have been met:

- The employee must have had actual notice of the notice requirement. (Proper posting of required employer FMLA notice will fulfill this requirement.)
- The employee's need for the leave and its approximate date must have been "clearly foreseeable" to the employee at least 30 days in advance.
- The employee is not being expected to adhere to a more stringent notice requirement than that applicable under the employer's policies for other leaves "such as leave for short duration."

---

[28] Regs. § 825.302(g).

- The employer's policies and procedures regarding advance notice of leave have been "uniformly applied in similar circumstances."

§ 2.14 Notice of Intent to Return to Work

The employer may require that an employee on FMLA leave give periodic notice regarding his or her status and intent to return to work, provided such a requirement is not "discriminatory" and takes into account "all of the relevant facts and circumstances related to the individual's leave situation." If the employee gives "unequivocal notice of intent not to return to work," the employer's FMLA obligations end. If the employee indicates that he or she "may be unable to return to work but expresses a continuing desire to do so," the employer's FMLA obligations remain intact.[29]

§ 2.15 Certification

An employer is entitled to require that the employee support any medical leave request with certification from the health care provider attesting to the serious health condition of the family member or the employee. The employer must, however, give written notice of this requirement to the employee. FMLA and the interim regulations provide that the healthcare provider's certification will be deemed sufficient if it contains the following information:

- ***Date of Onset.*** The date when the serious health condition commenced
- ***Duration.*** Its probable duration
- ***Diagnosis.*** A "diagnosis of the serious health condition"
- ***Treatment Prescribed.*** A "brief statement of the regimen of treatment prescribed for the condition by the health care provider"
- ***Hospitalization.*** Whether inpatient care will be required
- ***Statement of Need.*** If leave is required to enable the employee to care for a seriously ill family member, a statement that the family member requires the employee's assistance *or* that the employee's presence would be "beneficial or desirable" for the patient's care

---

[29] Regs. § 825.309. The interim regulations do not indicate what the employer may do in response to an employee's failure to communicate *any* intentions (or total failure to communicate at all); but it is likely that the employer's obligations would remain fully intact under such conditions.

- ***Estimate of Time.*** If leave is required to enable the employee to care for a seriously ill family member, a statement by the *employee* on the certification form of the kind of care the employee will provide and an estimate of the time needed to do so
- ***Employee's Inability to Work.*** If leave is required because of the employee's serious medical condition, a statement that the employee is unable to perform any kind of work or unable to perform the essential functions of the employee's position
- ***Medical Necessity.*** If intermittent leave or reduced leave schedule is sought, a statement of the medical necessity for that particular kind of leave, and the expected duration and schedule of the intermittent or reduced leave schedule [30]

Time to Provide Certification. The employee must provide the certification within the time frame established by the employer (which must be at least 15 days after the request) "unless it is not practicable under the circumstances to do so despite the employee's diligent, good faith efforts."[31] If a certification is incomplete, the employer must notify the employee and give the employee a reasonable opportunity to correct the deficiency.

Failure to Provide Certification. If an employee fails to provide timely certification for a foreseeable leave, the employer may deny the leave until the employee provides the certification. If the leave is not foreseeable, an employee must provide certification within the time frame requested (at least 15 days after the request), or as soon as reasonably possible; and if the employee fails to do so, the employer may deny continuation of the leave until the certification is provided.

§ 2.16 Second Opinion

If an employer has "reason to doubt" the validity of a health care provider's certification regarding the health condition of the employee or the employee's family member, the employer may, at its own expense, require that the employee get a second opinion from a second health care provider designated by the employer other than a health care provider who is "employed" by the employer "on a regular basis."[32]

---

[30] Regs. § 825.306. A sample certification form appears in Appendix C.

[31] Regs. § 825.305.

[32] FMLA § 103(c); Regs. § 825.307. The interim regulations seem to imply that the employer cannot routinely seek second FMLA certification opinions from health care providers (such as industrial clinics) with whom the employer regularly deals; but it does make exceptions for rural areas having few providers.

Reason to Doubt. Although *reason to doubt* is not defined either in FMLA or the interim regulations, it is possible that this provision was meant to require that the employer possess some objective basis for questioning the validity of the certification.

Christian Science Practitioner. If the certification is provided by a Christian Science practitioner, the employer may require that the employee or the employee's family member submit to an examination (not treatment) in order to obtain a second certification from a health care provider other than a Christian Science practitioner.[33]

§ 2.17 Third Opinion

If the second health care provider's opinion conflicts with that of the first health care provider, the employer may require (again, at its own expense) that the employee obtain a binding, third opinion from a third health care provider who is "approved jointly" by the employer and employee.

Joint Approval. The employer and employee are obligated to attempt in "good faith" to agree upon a third health care provider; if either party does not act in good faith, that party will be bound by the opinion contrary to its position.

§ 2.18 Recertification

An employer may require that an employee provide recertification on a "reasonable basis." A "reasonable basis" cannot be more often than every 30 days unless either:

- The employee requests an extension of the leave
- Circumstances described in the original certification have changed significantly
- The employer receives information casting doubt on the validity of the original certification

§ 2.19 "Fitness for Duty" Certification upon Return to Work

An employer may require, as a condition to an employee's returning to work from FMLA leave, that the employee provide certification from his

[33] Regs. § 825.118(b)(3).

or her health care provider that he or she is able to resume work, so long as *all* of the following conditions have been met:

- The employee's leave must have been occasioned by the employee's own serious health condition, *not* the birth or placement of a child or the need to care for a family member
- The employer must have in place a uniformly-applied policy requiring employees to produce such certifications under such conditions
- The employer has informed the employee, both generally and, more specifically, at or about the time the employee's leave commenced, that a fitness for duty certification would be required as a condition to the employee's return to work
- The fitness for duty certification relates only to the "particular health condition that caused the employee's need for FMLA leave"
- The requirement for furnishing of the certification does not violate state or local law or an applicable collective bargaining agreement

> [!] An employer requiring such certification must be careful not to violate the Americans with Disabilities Act requirement that the fitness-for-duty physical be clearly job-related.

Effect of Employee's Failure to Comply. An employer who has complied with all of the foregoing requirements may deny job restoration to an employee who fails to provide fitness-for-duty certification "until the certification is provided."[34]

§ 2.20 Substituted Leave

Under certain circumstances, an employee may choose *or* an employer may require that earned and accrued paid leave of various kinds be substituted for any part of the employee's otherwise unpaid FMLA leave period.[35]

> [!] The subject of substitution of paid leave is a matter involving terms and conditions of employment, and is therefore subject to collective bargaining. An employer's ability to compel substitution will likely be affected by the provisions of a collective bargaining agreement (for example, those provisions dealing with use of paid vacation time by employees).

Accrued Paid Vacation and Personal Leave Time. Any or all of the employee's accrued paid vacation and personal leave "time off" may be

---

[34] Regs. § 825.311(c).

[35] Regs. § 825.207.

substituted, at either the employer's or employee's option, for *any* qualified FMLA leave. The employer cannot impose any limitations on substitution of such time for these purposes.

Accrued Paid Medical/Sick Leave Time. At either the employer's or the employee's option, any or all of the employee's accrued paid medical/sick leave time may be substituted for FMLA leave caused by the *employee's* own serious health condition. The employer *may, but is not required to allow* such substitution for FMLA leave time occasioned by situations which would not normally be covered by the paid medical/sick leave program.

> ***Example:***
> The employer's policy excludes treatment for drug addiction from its paid sick leave coverage. An employee who takes FMLA leave for drug addiction treatment cannot substitute any accrued paid sick leave for the unpaid FMLA leave without the employer's permission.

Accrued Paid Family Leave Time. Where the employer maintains a program of paid family leave time off, the employee's accrued time under such a program may be substituted for FMLA leave at the employer's or the employee's request *provided* the condition giving rise to the leave is covered by the program.

> ***Example:***
> The employer's program allows use of accrued paid leave to care for a sick child, but not a sick parent. An employee taking FMLA leave to care for a seriously ill child would be entitled to substitute his or her accrued paid leave, but an employee tending to a sick parent would not.

§ 2.21 Designation of Leave

It is the employer's obligation to designate what leave, paid or unpaid, is being counted against an employee's FMLA entitlement, and to notify the employee that it has been so designated. The employer may only use information provided by the employee to make its designation, and the employer must notify the employee as soon as the designation has been made.

Unpaid Leave. An employee requesting unpaid leave must give the employer reasons that the leave is needed so that the employer can determine if the leave qualifies as FMLA leave.

Paid Leave. If an employee requests paid leave without giving a reason, and the employer denies it, the employee must provide more information to establish his or her entitlement, and in order that the employer "designate" it as FMLA leave.

Extending Accrued Paid Vacation Leave with Unpaid FMLA Leave. If an employee using accrued paid vacation leave (which does not qualify as FMLA leave) seeks to extend it with unpaid FMLA leave, the employee must state the reason, and the employer may count any part of the vacation time taken *after* the "FMLA-qualifying event" against the 12-week entitlement.

Substituting Accrued Paid Leave. If accrued paid leave is to be substituted or counted as FMLA leave, the decision to do so must be made at the time the employer determines that the leave qualifies. In other words, this decision must be made before the leave begins or is extended, unless the employer did not have sufficient information at that time. If leave is designated as FMLA leave after it commences, it can be designated FMLA leave retroactive to the portion of the leave time that qualified; but in no event may leave be designated as FMLA leave after the leave has ended.

CHAPTER 3

BENEFITS PROTECTED

§ 3.1 Job Restoration or Equivalent Job

An eligible employee who takes leave under FMLA is entitled to the following protections:

- **Job Restoration.** The employee must be restored to the same position he or she held at the time the leave began; or
- **Equivalent Position.** The employee must be placed into an equivalent position with equivalent employment benefits, pay, and other terms and conditions of employment.

§ 3.2 —Definition of Equivalent Position

Under the interim regulations, an *equivalent position* means a position with:

- The same pay
- The same benefits
- The same working conditions
- The same or substantially similar duties, responsibilities, privileges, and status
- Substantially equivalent skill, effort, responsibility, and authority
- Working at the same or a geographically proximate worksite, on the same shift or the same or equivalent work schedule

In the event that currency-type qualifications required for the position (for example, course attendance, license renewal, flight hour requirements) have lapsed during the leave, the employer must provide the employee with a reasonable opportunity to fulfill these requirements after returning to work. If there have been basic changes to the job during the employee's absence—such as closing of the worksite—the returning employee is entitled to be treated as if the employee had not been on leave when the event occurred, that is, to be treated as fellow workers were treated.[1]

§ 3.3 —Accrual of Benefits

An employee who is restored to work after taking a leave is entitled to benefits at the same level as were provided when the leave began. Such benefits include:

- Group life insurance
- Health insurance
- Disability insurance
- Sick leave
- Annual leave
- Educational benefits
- Pensions

Employees are *not* entitled to accrue additional benefits or seniority during unpaid FMLA leaves. On the other hand, wage or benefit increases which do not depend on the employee's seniority or accrual during the leave period (for example, cost of living raises) must be made effective upon their return to work.

An employee cannot be required to requalify for a benefit, such as life insurance, that might have lapsed during the leave. Moreover, the leave

[1] Regs. § 825.215.

time cannot be counted as a break in service for the purposes of denying vesting or eligibility under a pension or retirement plan.

[!] Employees (as well as their eligible dependents) who were covered by group health insurance programs at the time their FMLA leaves began cannot be subjected to waiting periods or new pre-existing condition restrictions upon their return. Similarly, they cannot be subjected to physical examinations or other conditions to requalify for life insurance benefits.

§ 3.4 —Maintenance of Health Coverage

The employer must maintain the employee's coverage under group health plans during FMLA leave. The employee is entitled both to

- The *same* benefit coverage during FMLA leave as that to which he or she was entitled prior to leave and to
- Any new or changed plan/benefits provided while the employee is on leave to the same extent as if the employee were not on leave.

Employee Premiums

The employer may require that any share of the total premiums paid by the employee prior to leave must continue to be paid by the employee during leave. If employee-paid premiums are raised or lowered, the employee on FMLA leave would be required to pay the new premium rates.

[!] While the Regulations allow for a variety of arrangements for payment of employee premiums, they do *not* permit the employer to require prepayment of employee premiums which will become due during the leave, and they do *not* allow the employer to "require more of an employee using FMLA leave than the employer requires of other employees on 'leave without pay.' "[2]

[!] Even if the employee's health insurance coverage lapses because of failure to pay premiums, upon return from leave the employee is nevertheless still entitled to full restoration of coverage without new conditions or preconditions.

Multi-Employer Health Plans

Employers must continue to make payments to multi-employer health plans on behalf of employees on FMLA leaves as though the employees

---

[2] Regs. § 825.210(c).

were continuously working, unless the plan contains a specific "FMLA provision" for maintenance of coverage through pooled employer contributions.

[!] These requirements override and nullify collective bargaining agreement provisions tying employer contribution obligations to hours or weeks worked per month and which, in effect, allow employers to discontinue contributions for employees who go on leaves of absence.

§ 3.5 —When Obligation to Maintain Coverage Ceases

The employer's obligation to maintain coverage (except as required by COBRA) ceases under the following circumstances:

- If the employee's premium payment is more than 30 days late
- When the employer learns of the employee's intent not to return from leave[3]
- If the employee fails to return from leave and employment is terminated
- When the employee exhausts FMLA leave entitlement
- If a "key employee"[4] does not return from leave when notified that a substantial or grievous economic injury will result from his or her reinstatement

§ 3.6 —Recovery of Premiums Paid by Employer

Health Benefit Plan Premiums

If an employee fails to return to work *for at least 30 calendar days* after his or her FMLA leave has expired, the employer may seek to recover all of the health benefit plan premiums it paid on the employee's behalf during the leave period, unless the employee's failure to return is caused by the continuation, recurrence, or onset of a serious health condition of the employee or a family member, or other circumstances beyond the employee's control.

Once the employee has returned to work and has worked 30 calendar days, the employer loses any right to collect the *employer's* share of health benefit plan premiums paid during the leave. Whether or not the employee

---

[3] See **Ch.2.**

[4] See § **3.13.**

returns to work, however, the employer may seek to collect any part of the *employee's* share of the health benefit plan premiums which the employee missed paying and which the employer paid on the employee's behalf.

Certification

If an employee is unable to return to work after FMLA leave because of the serious health condition of the employee or a family member, the employer may require the employee to provide medical certification of the serious health condition within 30 days. If the requested certification is not provided in a timely manner, the employer can take steps to recover its premium payments.

Effect of Substitution of Paid Leave

The employer may not recover its share of health insurance premium payments for any period of FMLA leave for which paid leave was substituted.

Other Plan Premiums

Where an employer pays premiums during an unpaid FMLA leave in order to ensure that an employee's life insurance, disability benefit, or other coverage does not lapse and can therefore be fully restored upon the employee's return, the employer may seek to collect any premium payments it made on the employee's behalf during the leave "whether or not the employee returns."[5]

§ 3.7 —Effect on FLSA Exempt Status

FMLA makes it clear that, as a general principle, employers do not have to pay employees for leave time taken pursuant to the Act. Congress recognized, however, that employers who docked salaried employees for time missed during certain leaves (for example, periodic intermittent leaves of less than a full day to receive medical attention) would destroy the employee's overtime pay exempt status under the Fair Labor Standards Act of 1938 (FLSA), thereby exposing the employer to possibly substantial liability for overtime premiums, retroactive and prospective. In response to this concern, FMLA expressly provides that "[w]here an employee is

---

[5] Regs. § 825.213(f).

otherwise exempt [from the overtime pay provisions of the FLSA], the compliance of an employer with [FMLA] by providing unpaid leave shall not affect the exempt status of the employee. . . ."[6]

[!] An employer should be careful, however, because this exception to the FLSA exemption requirements applies only to leave specifically provided for and required by FMLA. Therefore, if either the employee or the employer is not covered by FMLA or if any portion of the leave taken is "non-FMLA" leave (for example, taken pursuant to state law or to a more generous employer policy), docking of pay could jeopardize FLSA exempt status.

[!] The record-keeping provisions of the FMLA Regulations § 825.500 specify that, with respect to an exempt salaried employee taking FMLA leave on an intermittent or reduced leave schedule, the employer and the employee are to agree on the employee's normal schedule or average hours worked each week "and reduce their agreement to a written record" to be kept with other FMLA records.

§ 3.8 —Denial of Restoration

Under certain circumstances, an employer may deny job restoration to employees returning to work from a FMLA leave.

§ 3.9 —Employee Would Not Otherwise Have Been Employed

If an employer can show that an employee would not otherwise have been employed at the time reinstatement is requested (for example, due to a reduction in the workforce), the employer may deny job restoration.

§ 3.10 —Employment for a Fixed Term

An employer may also deny job restoration to an employee returning to work from a FMLA leave if the employee was hired for a specific or fixed term, or to perform work on a discrete project, and the term or project is completed.

---

[6] FMLA § 102(c).

§ 3.11 —Leave Obtained Through Fraud

An employee who fraudulently obtains FMLA leave is not protected by the FMLA's job restoration and maintenance of health benefits provisions.

§ 3.12 —Work for Others during Leave

If the employer has a uniformly applied policy prohibiting outside or supplemental employment, it may insist that employees abide by it even while on FMLA leave.[7] Presumably, employers may terminate (and therefore deny job restoration) to employees who violate such policies while on FMLA leave, provided they can show consistency in their treatment of employees otherwise violating the policy.

§ 3.13 —"Key" Employees

An employer may not deny leave, but may deny job restoration, to a "key" employee, if:

- The denial is necessary to prevent substantial and grievous economic injury to the employer's operations
- The employer has notified the employee of its intent to deny restoration
- Where leave is already in progress, the employee "elects not to return to employment after receiving such notice"[8]

A "key" employee is a "salaried employee who is among the highest paid 10 percent of the employees employed by the employer within 75 miles of the facility at which the employee is employed."

> [!] It is important to remember that key employees *are* entitled to take FMLA leaves, and they *may be* entitled to receive continuing health benefits during such a leave even though they may not be entitled to job restoration when the leave ends.

Calculating "Among the Highest Paid 10 Percent"

Include *all* employees employed by the employer within 75 miles of the employee's worksite, including salaried and nonsalaried and eligible and

---

[7] Regs. § 825.312(h).

[8] FMLA § 104(b).

noneligible employees; divide year-to-date earnings (as of the date of the request for leave) by weeks worked, including weeks in which paid leave was taken.

Economic Injury to Operations

The denial must be "necessary to prevent substantial and grievous economic injury" to the employer's operations.

[!] The relevant inquiry is the effect on operations of the company caused by *reinstating* the key employee to an equivalent position, not the effect on operations caused by his or her absence.

"Substantial and Grievous Economic Injury"

FMLA does not define "substantial and grievous economic injury." The regulations indicate that at least a substantial, long-term economic injury to the employer's operations must be shown. Like "serious health condition," this standard is very loose and subject to a wide range of interpretations and, therefore, uncertainty.

Notice of Key Employee Status

The employer must notify the employee in writing that he or she qualifies as a key employee at the time FMLA leave is requested or commences, or as soon as practicable. This written notice must state:

- The employee qualifies as a "key" employee
- The potential consequences to the employee if it is determined that grievous economic injury will flow from the employee's reinstatement

If the employer fails to provided timely notice, it will lose its right to deny restoration.[9]

Determination that Substantial and Grievous Economic Injury Will Result from Reinstatement

As soon as the employer makes a good faith determination that substantial and grievous economic injury will result from reinstatement of the key employee, the employer must notify the employee of the basis for its

---

[9] Regs. § 825.219(a).

determination and provide the employee a reasonable time in which to return to work.[10]

Request for Reinstatement

At the end of the leave period, the key employee is entitled to request reinstatement if he or she did not return to work in response to the employer's notice. The employer must then determine whether substantial and grievous economic injury will result, based on the facts at that time. If substantial and grievous economic injury would result, the employer must notify the employee in writing.

---

[10] Regs. § 825.219(b).

CHAPTER 4

OTHER OBLIGATIONS OF THE EMPLOYER

§ 4.1 Record-keeping Requirements

Employers are required to:

- Create records regarding their compliance with FMLA
- Keep the compliance records
- Preserve the compliance records for at least 3 years

No particular form or order of records is required, however.

§ 4.2 —Required Information

The records maintained by the employer must contain the following information:

- Basic payroll and employee identification data including:
  - Name
  - Address
  - Occupation

Rate or basis of pay and terms of compensation
Daily and weekly hours worked per pay period[1]
Additions to and deductions from wages
Total compensation

- The dates on which FMLA leave is taken
- If FMLA leave is taken for less than a full day, the hours of such leave
- Copies of all written notices of leave given by employees to the employer
- Copies of all written notices concerning FMLA given by the employer to employees
- Documents describing employee benefits or employer policies and practices regarding the taking of paid/unpaid leave
- Premium payments of employee benefits
- Records of any dispute regarding FMLA leave

§ 4.3 —Medical Records

The following records must be maintained separately and treated confidentially in accordance with the requirements of the ADA:

- Records relating to medical certifications and recertifications
- Records relating to medical histories of employees and their family members

However, as under the ADA, the following exceptions to confidentiality apply:

- Supervisors may be informed of work restrictions or accommodations
- First aid and safety personnel may be informed of any physical or medical condition of the employee which might require emergency treatment
- Government officials investigating compliance are to be provided relevant information on request.[2]

---

[1] This information need not be kept for employees who are not covered by or are exempt from FLSA. **BUT:** If they are not, the employer must, in the case of exempt employees taking intermittent or reduced leaves, maintain a written agreement with the employee regarding the employee's normal schedule or average hours worked each week. (See **[!]** in **Ch. 3** above)

[2] FMLA limits the authority of the DOL to require submission of records no more than once in any 12-month period unless it is investigating a complaint or unless it has "reasonable cause to believe a violation of the FMLA exists." Regs. § 825.500(a).

§ 4.4 Posting Requirement

Employers are required to post, and keep posted, in conspicuous places where notices for employees are customarily posted, a notice summarizing (or setting forth excerpts from) FMLA, and information relating to the filing of complaints.[3] Employers are also required to post translations if a significant portion of their workforce is not literate in English.

§ 4.5 —Failure to Post FMLA Notice

[WARN]

If an employer fails to post proper notice:

- A civil penalty ($100 for each offense) may be assessed if failure to post was willful
- The employer cannot take any adverse action against an employee, including denying FMLA leave, for failing to furnish the employer with advance notice of the need to take FMLA leave

Penalty

If a representative of the Department of Labor determines that an employer has willfully violated the posting requirement, and that the imposition of a civil penalty is appropriate, the representative may issue and serve a notice of penalty (in person or by certified mail).

Review

An employer may petition the Wage and Hour Regional Administrator to review a penalty assessment. The petition must be mailed to the Administrator within 15 days of receipt of the notice of penalty. The employer can request an oral hearing, which can be conducted by telephone.

Failure to Pay Penalty

If an employer does not pay the amount of the penalty after a final order is entered, the Secretary of Labor may file suit to recover the amount of

---

[3] FMLA § 109. A copy of an acceptable notice form is set out in **App. A.** The Regulations require that, if duplicated, the posted notice must be no smaller than 8.5 by 11 inches. Regs. § 825.300(a).

the penalty, interest, and additional penalties assessed as a result of the failure to pay.

§ 4.6 Other Written Notices

If an employer provides written guidance to employees regarding employment benefits or leave rights (for example, in an employment handbook), the employer must include in it all relevant information concerning the employer's policies with respect to FMLA and the employee's rights and obligations under FMLA.

§ 4.7 —Notice to Employees Requesting Leave

Even if the employer does not have written policies or sources of information, the employer is still obligated to provide written guidance concerning all of the employee's FMLA rights and obligations to any employee who requests a FMLA leave. (The employer may provide copies of the "FMLA Fact Sheet" which is available from the Wage and Hour Division of the Department of Labor.)[4] In addition, the employer must provide the employee with notice (not necessarily written) **at the time the employee requests leave** detailing the specific expectations and obligations of the employee and explaining any consequences of a failure to meet these obligations. This notice must include, where applicable:

- That the leave will be counted against the employee's annual FMLA leave entitlement
- Any requirement that the employee furnish medical certification of a serious health condition, and the consequences of his or her failure to furnish such a certification
- The employee's right to substitute paid leave for FMLA leave, whether the employer will require such substitution, and the conditions related to any substitution
- Any requirement that the employee make premium payments necessary to maintain health benefits and the arrangements for payment of such premiums
- Any requirement the employee will have to present fitness-for-duty certification in order to return to work at the end of the leave
- The employee's right to be restored to the same or an equivalent job upon return from leave or, in the alternative, an explanation of the

[4] Regs. § 825.301.

employee's "key employee" status, that job restoration may be denied following the leave, and an explanation of the conditions required for such denial

- The employee's potential liability, should he or she not return from leave, to reimburse the employer for health insurance premiums paid on the employee's behalf during unpaid FMLA leave

CHAPTER 5

PROHIBITED CONDUCT, ENFORCEMENT PROCEDURES, AND REMEDIES

CONDUCT

§ 5.1 Prohibited Conduct

The FMLA makes it unlawful for an employer to:

- **Interfere or Restrain.** Interfere with, restrain, or deny the exercise or attempt to exercise FMLA rights
- **Discharge or Discriminate.** Discharge or discriminate against any individual for opposing any unlawful practice under FMLA
- **Retaliate.** Discharge or discriminate in any way against any individual because the individual has:

- Filed a charge, or caused a "proceeding" to be instituted under or related to FMLA
- Given or "is about to give" information in connection with an "inquiry or proceeding" relating to a right provided by FMLA
- Testified, or "is about to testify, in any inquiry or proceeding" relating to a right provided by FMLA

Examples

Discouraging or attempting to discourage an employee from using FMLA leave constitutes a form of prohibited interference.

Transferring employees from one worksite to another for the purpose of rendering them ineligible for leave would be prohibited.

Where the employer has a general practice of allowing employees on unpaid leaves to maintain all benefits (not only health benefits), it would be unlawful for the employer to deny such benefits to employees on unpaid FMLA leaves.

If the employer does not normally require written notice or certification for use of *paid* leaves, the employer cannot require such notice or certification to an employee who substitutes paid leave for FMLA leave.

When making performance evaluations and considering employees for promotion, assigning a negative factor to absence attributable to FMLA leave would not be permissible.

[!] FMLA leave cannot be counted as an absence under "no fault" attendance policies.[1]

ENFORCEMENT

§ 5.2 Enforcement by an Employee

An employee has two options for proceeding against an employer under FMLA:

- **Lawsuit.** The employee may file suit on his or her own on behalf and on behalf of all other similarly situated employees.
- **Complaint.** The employee, or another person on the employee's behalf, may file a complaint in person, by mail, or by telephone[2] with the

---

[1] Regs. § 825.220(c).

[2] Regs. § 825.401(a).

Secretary of Labor. Such complaints are handled by local offices of the Wage & Hour Division of the Employment Standards Administration, U.S. Department of Labor, the same Division which deals with federal minimum wage and overtime matters under the Fair Labor Standards Act.

Note: Unlike claims arising under Title VII, the Americans With Disabilities Act and the Age Discrimination in Employment Act, claims alleging violation of FMLA are *not* subject to EEOC jursidiction.

§ 5.3 Suits by Employees and Secretary of Labor

Court Jurisdiction

Either the employee or the Secretary of Labor may file suit alleging violation of FMLA in federal or state court. If the employee files the suit, either court may award damages and/or equitable relief such as reinstatement of employment, promotion, and so forth. The Secretary of Labor is permitted to seek equitable relief only in federal court (though the Secretary may seek damages in either).

Effect of Secretary of Labor's Suit on Employee's Rights

Whenever the Secretary of Labor files a suit alleging FMLA violation, any affected employee loses the right to pursue an individual suit, whether or not it has already been filed.[3]

§ 5.4 Limitations Period

A lawsuit under FMLA (whether brought by an employee or the Secretary of Labor) must be filed within two years of the violation, unless the violation is "willful," in which case it must be brought within three years of the violation.[4]

Commencement of Action

A lawsuit is commenced under FMLA on the date the complaint is filed in court.

---

[3] FMLA § 107(a)(4).

[4] FMLA § 107(c).

"Willful" Violation. Although the term *willful* is not defined in FMLA, this term probably will have the same meaning as it has in the Age Discrimination in Employment Act, that is, a violation will be deemed willful if the employer knows its conduct violates the law, or if the employer acts with reckless disregard as to whether its conduct is in violation of the law.

Filing Complaint with Secretary. A complaint should be filed with the Secretary of Labor within a reasonable time of when the employee discovers that his or her FMLA rights have been violated. In no event may a complaint be filed with the Secretary more than two years after the violation occurred (or three years in the case of a willful violation).[5]

§ 5.5 Private Settlement Agreements

It is not clear whether employers and employees will be allowed to enter into enforceable private agreements to settle claims arising under FMLA. FMLA is enforced by the Department of Labor, and incorporates the procedures used to process complaints under the Fair Labor Standards Act (FLSA). Under FLSA, employers generally cannot enter into unsupervised settlements (settlements not approved by a court or the Department of Labor). Thus, in light of the incorporation of FLSA's enforcement procedures, employers also may be prohibited from entering into unsupervised settlement agreements under FMLA.

REMEDIES

§ 5.6 Suit Brought by Employee

An employee who brings suit and proves that his or her rights under FMLA have been violated is entitled to:

Damages consisting of:

Lost Wages and Benefits. Wages, salary, benefits, or other compensation lost as a result of the violation; *or*

Losses Resulting from the Violation. If no wages, salary, benefits, or other compensation is lost because of the violation, any actual monetary losses sustained by the employee as a "direct result" of the violation, such as the cost incurred by the employee in providing care

---

[5] Regs. § 825.401(a).

to the new child or the seriously ill relative, up to a sum equal to 12 weeks of the employee's wages or salary; *and*, in either case,

Interest. Interest at the prevailing rate on the amount of damages recovered; *and*

Liquidated Damages. An amount equal to the sum of damages and interest awarded, *unless* the employer proves to the satisfaction of the court that it acted in good faith and had reasonable grounds for believing that its conduct was not a violation of FMLA *and* if the court, in its discretion, declines to award liquidated damages; *and*

Equitable Relief. Appropriate equitable relief, including employment, reinstatement, and promotion; *and*

Fees and Costs. Reasonable attorney's fee, expert witness fees, and other costs of suit.

§ 5.7 Suit Brought by Secretary of Labor

If a successful suit is brought by the Secretary of Labor, the employer is liable for:

Damages consisting of:

Lost Wages and Benefits. Wages, salary, benefits, or other compensation lost by employees as a result of the employer's violation of FMLA; *or*

Losses Resulting from the Violation. If no wages, salary, benefits, or other compensation has been lost because of the violation, any actual monetary losses sustained by employees as a direct result of the violation such as the costs they incurred in providing care to new children or seriously ill relatives, up to a sum equal to 12 weeks of the employee's wages or salary; *and*, in either case,

Interest. Interest at the prevailing rate on the amount of damages recovered; *and*

Liquidated damages. An amount equal to the sum of damages and interest awarded, *unless* the employer proves "to the satisfaction of the court" that it acted in "good faith" and had "reasonable grounds" for believing that its conduct was not a violation of FMLA *and* if the court, in its discretion, declines to award liquidated damages.

Note: Any sums recovered by the Secretary of Labor are to be held in a special deposit account and paid by the Secretary to the aggrieved employee; any sums not paid out to employees within 3 years are to be deposited into the U.S. Treasury.

If the Secretary of Labor brings the suit in federal district court, he may also obtain:

Injunctive Relief in the form of an order restraining the employer from witholding of wages, salary, employment benefits, or other compensation, plus interest; *and*

Equitable Relief including employment, reinstatement, and promotion, where appropriate.

CHAPTER 6

MISCELLANEOUS PROVISIONS

§ 6.1 Effective Date

FMLA became effective on August 5, 1993, except for employees covered by a collective bargaining agreement, in which case FMLA became effective on the earlier of:

- The termination of the collective bargaining agreement
- February 5, 1994.

§ 6.2 Effect on Employment Discrimination Laws

FMLA does not modify or affect any federal or state law prohibiting discrimination on the basis of race, religion, color, national origin, sex, age, or disability.[1] If an employer violates FMLA and an antidiscrimination statute, the employee may recover under either or both of the violated statutes.

[1] FMLA § 401(a).

§ 6.3 Interaction with the Americans with Disabilities Act (ADA)

If an employee is a qualified person with a disability within the meaning of the Americans with Disabilities Act (ADA), the employer must provide the employee with reasonable accommodation for the disability *and* comply with FMLA.

- An employer may not require that an employee take a job (which constitutes a reasonable accommodation for the employee's disability) in lieu of FMLA leave; but the employer may be obligated under the ADA to *offer* the employee the opportunity to take such a position.[2]
- An employee who has exhausted FMLA leave entitlement *may* be entitled to additional leave or intermittent leave (a modified work schedule) as a reasonable accommodation under ADA.
- While FMLA allows restoration upon return from leave to an *equivalent* position, an employee returning from leave given as reasonable accommodation under ADA is entitled to the *same* position upon return (if it still exists.[3]

§ 6.4 Relationship to State Leave Laws

FMLA does not supersede any state or local law which provides greater family or medical leave rights than FMLA.[4] An employer must comply with whichever statute provides greater leave rights to the employee. However, if a single leave qualifies both as FMLA leave and as leave cognizable under the applicable state law, it can generally be charged against the employee's leave entitlement under both laws.

§ 6.5 Effect on Collective Bargaining Agreements or Benefit Programs

If a collective bargaining agreement or employee benefit program provides greater family and medical leave rights than FMLA, an employer must provide employees with the more generous leave.

---

[2] *See also* **Ch. 2.**

[3] See discussion of ADA considerations of **Ch. 2.**

[4] FMLA § 401(b).

[!] However, the rights established by the FMLA cannot be diminished by less protective provisions in a collective bargaining agreement or employee benefit program.

If an employer provides greater unpaid leave than that required by FMLA, the employer is not obligated to extend additional rights such as maintenance of health benefits (unless required by COBRA) to the additional leave period (beyond 12 weeks) not covered by FMLA.

§ 6.6 Amendment of Leave Policies or Benefit Programs

FMLA does not prohibit an employer from amending its leave policies or benefit programs (provided the amended provisions comply with FMLA).

§ 6.7 Special Rules for School Employees

Section 108 of FMLA contains a number of special rules applicable to employees of "local educational agencies," defined by the interim regulations[5] as including public school boards and both private and public elementary and secondary schools. In brief, these rules (which do not apply to employees of colleges, universities, trade schools, or preschools) limit the rights of certain intructional employees (teachers, athletic coaches, driving instructors, and special education assistants) working with small classes or individual students to take intermittent leaves, reduced leave schedules, or leaves during the last few weeks of an academic term. In addition, FMLA provides that the manner by which *any* employee of a local educational agency is to be restored to an equivalent position at the end of a FMLA leave is to be determined in accordance with established policies, practices, and collective bargaining agreements.[6]

---

[5] Regs. §§ 825.600–800.604.

[6] FMLA § 108(e). The interim regulations provide, however, that such policies and collective bargaining agreements "must provide substantially the same protections as provided in [FMLA] for reinstated employees." Regs. § 825.604.

CHAPTER 7

STATUTE AND REGULATIONS

§ 7.1 Introduction

This unit sets out:

- The text of FMLA (Public Law 103-3, 29 U.S.C. §§ 2601–2654).
- Interim Final Regulations Issued by the Department of Labor Wage and Hour Division on June 4, 1993 (29 C.F.R. Part 825).

§ 7.2 FMLA: Statutory Provisions

TEXT OF PUBLIC LAW 103-3

An Act

To grant family and temporary medical leave under certain circumstances.

Be it enacted by the Senate and House of Representatives of the United States of America in Congress assembled,

SECTION 1. SHORT TITLE; TABLE OF CONTENTS.

(a) Short Title.—This Act may be cited as the "Family and Medical Leave Act of 1993."

(b) Table of Contents.—The table of contents is as follows:

TITLE VI—SENSE OF CONGRESS

Sec. 601. Sense of Congress.

SECTION 2. FINDINGS AND PURPOSES.

(a) Findings.—Congress finds that—

(1) the number of single-parent households and two-parent households in which the single parent or both parents work is increasing significantly;

(2) it is important for the development of children and the family unit that fathers and mothers be able to participate in early childrearing and the care of family members who have serious health conditions;

(3) the lack of employment policies to accommodate working parents can force individuals to choose between job security and parenting.

(4) there is inadequate job security for employees who have serious health conditions that prevent them from working for temporary periods;

(5) due to the nature of the roles of men and women in our society, the primary responsibility for family caretaking often falls on women, and such responsibility affects the working lives of women more than it affects the working lives of men; and

(6) employment standards that apply to one gender only have serious potential for encouraging employers to discriminate against employees and applicants for employment who are of that gender.

(b) Purposes.—It is the purpose of this Act—

(1) to balance the demands of the workplace with the needs of families, to promote the stability and economic security of families, and to promote national interests in preserving family integrity;

(2) to entitle employees to take reasonable leave for medical reasons, for the birth or adoption of a child, and for the care of a child, spouse, or parent who has a serious health condition;

(3) to accomplish the purposes described in paragraphs (1) and (2) in a manner that accommodates the legitimate interests of employers;

(4) to accomplish the purposes described in paragraphs (1) and (2) in a manner that, consistent with the Equal Protection Clause of the Fourteenth Amendment, minimizes the potential for employment discrimination on the basis of sex by ensuring generally that leave is available for eligible medical reasons (including maternity-related disability) and for compelling family reasons, on a gender-neutral basis; and

(5) to promote the goal of equal employment opportunity for women and men, pursuant to such clause.

TITLE I—GENERAL REQUIREMENTS FOR LEAVE

SEC. 101. DEFINITIONS.

As used in this title:

(1) Commerce.—The terms "commerce" and "industry or activity affecting commerce" mean any activity, business, or industry in commerce or in which a labor dispute would hinder or obstruct commerce or the free flow of commerce, and include "commerce" and any "industry affecting commerce," as defined in paragraphs (1) and (3) of section 501 of the Labor Management Relations Act, 1947 (29 U.S.C. 142(1) and (3)).

(2) Eligible employee.—

(A) In general.—The term "eligible employee" means an employee who has been employed—

(i) for at least 12 months by the employer with respect to whom leave is requested under section 102; and

(ii) for at least 1,250 hours of service with such employer during the previous 12-month period.

(B) Exclusions.—The term "eligible employee" does not include—

(i) any Federal officer or employee covered under subchapter V of chapter 63 of title 5, United States Code (as added by title II of this Act); or

(ii) any employee of an employer who is employed at a worksite at which such employer employs less than 50 employees if the total number of employees employed by that employer within 75 miles of that worksite is less than 50.

(C) Determination.—For purposes of determining whether an employee meets the hours of service requirement specified in subparagraph (A)(ii), the legal standards established under section 7 of the Fair Labor Standards Act of 1938 (29 U.S.C. 207) shall apply.

(3) Employ; employee; state.—The terms "employ," "employee," and "State" have the same meanings given such terms in subsections (c), (e), and (g) of section 3 of the Fair Labor Standards Act of 1938 (29 U.S.C. 203(c), (e), and (g)).

(4) Employer.—

(A) In general.—The term "employer"—

(i) means any person engaged in commerce or in any industry or activity affecting commerce who employs 50 or more employees for each working day during each of twenty or more calendar workweeks in the current or preceding calendar year;

(ii) includes—

(I) any person who acts, directly or indirectly, in the interest of an employer to any of the employees of such employer; and

(II) any successor in interest of an employer; and

(iii) includes any "public agency," as defined in section 3(x) of the Fair Labor Standards Act of 1938 (29 U.S.C. 203(x)).

(B) Public agency.—For purposes of subparagraph (A)(iii), a public agency shall be considered to be a person engaged in commerce or in an industry or activity affecting commerce.

(5) Employment benefits.—The term "employment benefits" means all benefits provided or made available to employees by an employer, including group life insurance, health insurance, disability insurance, sick leave, annual leave, educational benefits, and pensions, regardless of whether such benefits are provided by a practice or written policy of an employer or through an "employee benefit plan," as defined in section 3(3) of the Employee Retirement Income Security Act of 1974 (29 U.S.C. 1002(3)).

(6) Health care provider.—The term "health care provider" means—

(A) a doctor of medicine or osteopathy who is authorized to practice medicine or surgery (as appropriate) by the State in which the doctor practices; or

(B) any other person determined by the Secretary to be capable of providing health care services.

(7) Parent.—The term "parent" means the biological parent of an employee or an individual who stood in loco parentis to an employee when the employee was a son or daughter.

(8) Person.—The term "person" has the same meaning given such term in section 3(a) of the Fair Labor Standards Act of 1938 (29 U.S.C. 203(a)).

(9) Reduced leave schedule.—The term "reduced leave schedule" means a leave schedule that reduces the usual number of hours per workweek, or hours per workday, of an employee.

(10) Secretary.—The term "Secretary" means the Secretary of Labor.

(11) Serious health condition.—The term "serious health condition" means an illness, injury, impairment, or physical or mental condition that involves—

(A) inpatient care in a hospital, hospice, or residential medical care facility; or

(B) continuing treatment by a health care provider.

(12) Son or daughter.—The term "son or daughter" means a biological, adopted, or foster child, a step-child, a legal ward, or a child of a person standing in loco parentis, who is—

(A) under 18 years of age; or

(B) 18 years of age or older and incapable of self-care because of a mental or physical disability.

(13) Spouse.—The term "spouse" means a husband or wife, as the case may be.

SEC. 102. LEAVE REQUIREMENT.

(a) In General.—

(1) Entitlement to leave.—Subject to section 103, an eligible employee shall be entitled to a total of 12 workweeks of leave during any 12-month period for one or more of the following:

(A) Because of the birth of a son or daughter of the employee and in order to care for such son or daughter.

(B) Because of the placement of a son or daughter with the employee for adoption or foster care.

(C) In order to care for the spouse, or a son, daughter, or parent, of the employee, if such spouse, son, daughter, or parent has a serious health condition.

(D) Because of a serious health condition that makes the employee unable to perform the functions of the position of such employee.

(2) Expiration of entitlement.—The entitlement to leave under subparagraphs (A) and (B) of paragraph (1) for a birth or placement of a son or daughter shall expire at the end of the 12-month period beginning on the date of such birth or placement.

(b) Leave Taken Intermittently or on a Reduced Leave Schedule.—

(1) In general.—Leave under subparagraph (A) or (B) of subsection (a)(1) shall not be taken by an employee intermittently or on a reduced leave schedule unless the employee and the employer of the employee agree otherwise. Subject to paragraph (2), subsection (e)(2), and section 103(b)(5), leave under subparagraph (C) or (D) of subsection (a)(1) may be taken intermittently or on a reduced leave schedule when medically necessary. The taking of leave intermittently or on a reduced leave schedule pursuant to this paragraph shall not result in a reduction in the total amount of leave to which the employee is entitled under subsection (a) beyond the amount of leave actually taken.

(2) Alternative position.—If an employee requests intermittent leave, or leave on a reduced leave schedule, under subparagraph (C) or (D) of subsection (a)(1), that is foreseeable based on planned medical treatment, the employer may require such employee to transfer temporarily to an

available alternative position offered by the employer for which the employee is qualified and that—

(A) has equivalent pay and benefits; and

(B) better accommodates recurring periods of leave than the regular employment position of the employee.

(c) Unpaid Leave Permitted.—Except as provided in subsection (d), leave granted under subsection (a) may consist of unpaid leave. Where an employee is otherwise exempt under regulations issued by the Secretary pursuant to section 13(a)(1) of the Fair Labor Standards Act of 1938 (29 U.S.C. 213(a)(1)), the compliance of an employer with this title by providing unpaid leave shall not affect the exempt status of the employee under such section.

(d) Relationship to Paid Leave.—

(1) Unpaid leave.—If an employer provides paid leave for fewer than 12 workweeks, the additional weeks of leave necessary to attain the 12 workweeks of leave required under this title may be provided without compensation.

(2) Substitution of paid leave.—

(A) In general.—An eligible employee may elect, or an employer may require the employee, to substitute any of the accrued paid vacation leave, personal leave, or family leave of the employee for leave provided under subparagraph (A), (B), or (C) of subsection (a)(1) for any part of the 12-week period of such leave under such subsection.

(B) Serious health condition.—An eligible employee may elect, or an employer may require the employee, to substitute any of the accrued paid vacation leave, personal leave, or medical or sick leave of the employee for leave provided under subparagraph (C) or (D) of subsection (a)(1) for any part of the 12-week period of such leave under such subsection, except that nothing in this title shall require an employer to provide paid sick leave or paid medical leave in any situation in which such employer would not normally provide any such paid leave.

(e) Foreseeable Leave.—

(1) Requirement of notice.—In any case in which the necessity for leave under subparagraph (A) or (B) of subsection (a)(1) is foreseeable based on

an expected birth or placement, the employee shall provide the employer with not less than 30 days' notice, before the date the leave is to begin, of the employee's intention to take leave under such subparagraph, except that if the date of the birth or placement requires leave to begin in less than 30 days, the employee shall provide such notice as is practicable.

(2) Duties of employee.—In any case in which the necessity for leave under subparagraph (C) or (D) of subsection (a)(1) is foreseeable based on planned medical treatment, the employee—

(A) shall make a reasonable effort to schedule the treatment so as not to disrupt unduly the operations of the employer, subject to approval of the health care provider of the employee or the health care provider of the son, daughter, spouse, or parent of the employee, as appropriate; and

(B) shall provide the employer with not less than 30 days' notice, before the date the leave is to begin, of the employee's intention to take leave under such subparagraph, except that if the date of the treatment requires leave to begin in less than 30 days, the employee shall provide such notice as is practicable.

(f) Spouses Employed by the Same Employer.—In any case in which a husband and wife entitled to leave under subsection (a) are employed by the same employer, the aggregate number of workweeks of leave to which both may be entitled may be limited to 12 workweeks during any 12-month period, if such leave is taken—

(1) under subparagraph (A) or (B) or subsection (a)(1); or

(2) to care for a sick parent under subparagraph (C) of such subsection.

SEC. 103. CERTIFICATION.

(a) In General.—An employer may require that a request for leave under subparagraph (C) or (D) of section 102(a)(1) be supported by a certification issued by the health care provider of the eligible employee or of the son, daughter, spouse, or parent of the employee, as appropriate. The employee shall provide, in a timely manner, a copy of such certification to the employer.

(b) Sufficient Certification.—Certification provided under subsection (a) shall be sufficient if it states—

(1) the date on which the serious health condition commenced;

(2) the probable duration of the condition;

(3) the appropriate medical facts within the knowledge of the health care provider regarding the condition;

(4)(A) for purposes of leave under section 102(a)(1)(C), a statement that the eligible employee is needed to care for the son, daughter, spouse, or parent and an estimate of the amount of time that such employee is needed to care for the son, daughter, spouse, or parent; and

(B) for purposes of leave under section 102(a)(1)(D), a statement that the employee is unable to perform the functions of the position of the employee;

(5) in the case of certification for intermittent leave, or leave on a reduced leave schedule, for planned medical treatment, the dates of which such treatment is expected to be given and the duration of such treatment;

(6) in the case of certification for intermittent leave, or leave on a reduced leave schedule, under section 102(a)(1)(D), a statement of the medical necessity for the intermittent leave or leave on a reduced leave schedule, and the expected duration of the intermittent leave or reduced leave schedule; and

(7) in the case of certification for intermittent leave, or leave on a reduced schedule, under section 102(a)(1)(C), a statement that the employee's intermittent leave or leave on a reduced leave schedule is necessary for the care of the son, daughter, parent or spouse who has a serious health condition, or will assist in their recovery, and the expected duration and schedule of the intermittent leave or reduced leave schedule.

(c) Second Opinion.—

(1) In general.—In any case in which the employer has reason to doubt the validity of the certification provided under subsection (a) for leave under subparagraph (C) or (D) of section 102(a)(1), the employer may require, as the expense of the employer, that the eligible employee obtain the opinion of a second health care provider designated or approved by the employer concerning any information certified under subsection (b) for such leave.

(2) Limitation.—A health care provider designated or approved under paragraph (1) shall not be employed on a regular basis by the employer.

(d) Resolution of Conflicting Opinions.—

(1) In general.—In any case in which the second opinion described in subsection (c) differs from the opinion in the original certification provided under subsection (a), the employer may require, at the expense of the employer, that the employee obtain the opinion of a third health care provider designated or approved jointly by the employer and the employee concerning the information certified under subsection (b).

(2) Finality.—The opinion of the third health care provider concerning the information certified under subsection (b) shall be considered to be final and shall be binding on the employer and the employee.

(e) Subsequent Recertification.—The employer may require that the eligible employee obtain subsequent recertifications on a reasonable basis.

SEC. 104. EMPLOYMENT AND BENEFITS PROTECTION.

(a) Restoration to Position.—

(1) In general.—Except as provided in subsection (b), any eligible employee who takes leave under section 102 for the intended purpose of the leave shall be entitled, on return from such leave—

(A) to be restored by the employer to the position of the employment held by the employee when the leave commenced; or

(B) to be restored to an equivalent position with equivalent employment benefits, pay, and other terms and conditions of employment.

(2) Loss of benefits.—The taking of leave under section 102 shall not result in the loss of any employment benefit accrued prior to the date on which the leave commenced.

(3) Limitations.—Nothing in this section shall abe construed to entitle any restored employee to—

(A) the accrual of any seniority or employment benefits during any period of leave; or

(B) any right, benefit, or position of employment other than any right, benefit or position to which the employee would have been entitled had the employee not taken the leave.

(4) Certification.—As a condition of restoration under paragraph (1) for an employee who has taken leave under section 102(a)(1)(D), the employer may have a uniformly applied practice or policy that requires each such employee to receive certification from the health care provider of the employee that the employee is able to resume work, except that nothing in this paragraph shall supersede a valid State or local law or a collective bargaining agreement that governs the return to work of such employees.

(5) Construction.—Nothing in this subsection shall be construed to prohibit an employer from requiring an employee on leave under section 102 to report periodically to the employer on the status and intention of the employee to return to work.

(b) Exemption Concerning Certain Highly Compensated Employees.—

(1) Denial of restoration.—An employer may deny restoration under subsection (a) to any eligible employee described in paragraph (2) if—

(A) such denial is necessary to prevent substantial and grievous economic injury to the operations of the employer;

(B) the employer notifies the employee of the intent of the employer to deny restoration on such basis at the time the employer determines that such injury would occur; and

(C) in any case in which the leave has commenced, the employee elects not to return to employment after receiving such notice.

(2) Affected employees.—An eligible employee described in paragraph (1) is a salaried eligible employee who is among the highest paid 10 percent of the employees employed by the employer within 75 miles of the facility at which the employee is employed.

(c) Maintenance of Health Benefits.—

(1) Coverage.—Except as provided in paragraph (2), during any period that an eligible employee takes leave under section 102, the employer shall maintain coverage under any "group health plan" (as defined to section 5000(b)(1) of the Internal Revenue Code of 1986) for the duration of such leave at the level and under the conditions coverage would have been

provided if the employee had continued in employment continuously for the duration of such leave.

(2) Failure to return from leave.—The employer may recover the premium that the employer paid for maintaining coverage for the employee under such group health plan during any period of unpaid leave under section 102 if—

(A) the employee fails to return from leave under section 102 after the period of leave to which the employee is entitled has expired; and

(B) the employee fails to return to work for a reason other than—

(i) the continuation, recurrence, or onset of a serious health condition that entitles the employee to leave under subparagraph (C) or (D) of section 102(a)(1); or

(ii) other circumstances beyond the control of the employee.

(3) Certification.—

(A) Issuance.—An employer may require that a claim that an employee is unable to return to work because of the continuation, recurrence, or onset of the serious health condition described in paragraph (2)(B)(i) be supported by—

(i) a certification issued by the health care provider of the son, daughter, spouse, or parent of the employee, as appropriate, in the case of an employee unable to return to work because of a condition specified in section 102(a)(1)(C); or

(ii) a certification by the health care provider of the eligible employee, in the case of an employee unable to return to work because of a condition specified in section 102(a)(1)(D).

(B) Copy.—The employee shall provide, in a timely manner, a copy of such certification to the employer.

(C) Sufficiency of certification.—

(i) Leave due to serious health condition of employee.—The certification described in subparagraph (A)(ii) shall be sufficient if the certification states that a serious health condition prevented the employee from being able to perform the functions of the position of the employee on the date that the leave of the employee expired.

(ii) Leave due to serious health condition of family member.—The certification described in subparagraph (A)(i) shall be sufficient if the certification states that the employee is needed to care for the son, daughter, spouse, or parent who has a serious health condition on the date that the leave of the employee expired.

SEC.105. PROHIBITED ACTS.

(a) Interference With Rights.—

(1) Exercise of rights.—It shall be unlawful for any employer to interfere with, restrain, or deny the exercise of or the attempt to exercise, any right provided under this title.

(2) Discrimination.—It shall be unlawful for any employer to discharge or in any other manner discriminate against any individual for opposing any practice made unlawful by this title.

(b) Interference With Proceedings or Inquiries.—It shall be unlawful for any person to discharge or in any other manner discriminate against any individual because such individual—

(1) has filed any charge, or has instituted or caused to be instituted any proceeding, under or related to this title;

(2) has given, or is about to give, any information in connection with any inquiry or proceeding relating to any right provided under this title; or

(3) has testified, or is about to testify, in any inquiry or proceeding relating to any right provided under this title.

SEC. 106. INVESTIGATIVE AUTHORITY.

(a) In General.—To ensure compliance with the provisions of this title, or any regulation or order issued under this title, the Secretary shall have, subject to subsection (c), the investigative authority provided under section 11(a) of the Fair Labor Standards Act of 1938 (29 U.S.C. 211(a)).

(b) Obligation to Keep and Preserve Records.—Any employer shall make, keep, and preserve records pertaining to compliance with this title in accordance with section 11(c) of the Fair Labor Standards Act of 1938 (29 U.S.C. 211(c)) and in accordance with regulations issued by the Secretary.

(c) Required Submissions Generally Limited to an Annual Basis.—The Secretary shall not under the authority of this section require any employer or any plan, fund or program to submit to the Secretary any books or records more than once during any 12-month period, unless the Secretary has reasonable cause to believe there may exist a violation of this title or any regulation or order issued pursuant to section 107(b).

(d) Subpoena Powers.—For the purposes of any investigation provided for in this section, the Secretary shall have the subpoena authority provided for under section 9 of the Fair Labor Standards Act of 1938 (29 U.S.C. 209).

SEC. 107. ENFORCEMENT.

(a) Civil Action by Employees.—

(1) Liability.—Any employer who violates section 105 shall be liable to any eligible employee affected—

(A) for damages equal to—

(i) the amount of—

(I) any wages, salary, employment benefits, or other compensation denied or lost to such employee by reason of the violation; or

(II) in a case in which wages, salary, employment benefits, or other compensation have not been denied or lost to the employee, any actual monetary losses sustained by the employee as a direct result of the violation, such as the cost of providing care, up to a sum equal to 12 weeks of wages or salary for the employee;

(ii) the interest on the amount described in clause (i) calculated at the prevailing rate; and

(iii) an additional amount as liquidated damages equal to the sum of the amount described in clause (i) and the interest described in clause (ii), except that if an employer who has violated section 105 proves to the satisfaction of the court that the act or omission which violated section 105 was in good faith and that the employer had reasonable grounds for believing that the act or omission was not a violation of section 105, such court may, in the discretion of the court, reduce the amount of the liability to the amount and interest determined under clauses (i) and (ii), respectively; and

(B) for such equitable relief as may be appropriate, including employment, reinstatement, and promotion.

(2) Right of action.—An action to recover the damages or equitable relief prescribed in paragraph (1) may be maintained against any employer (including a public agency) in any Federal or State court of competent jurisdiction by any one or more employees for and in behalf of—

(A) the employees; or

(B) The employees and other employees similarly situated.

(3) Fees and costs.—The court in such an action shall, in addition to any judgment awarded to the plaintiff, allow a reasonable attorney's fee, reasonable expert witness fees, and other costs of the action to be paid by the defendant.

(4) Limitations.—The right provided by paragraph (2) to bring an action by or on behalf of any employee shall terminate—

(A) on the filing of a complaint by the Secretary in an action under subsection (d) in which restraint is sought of any further delay in the payment of the amount described in paragraph (1)(A) to such employee by an employer responsible under paragraph (1) for the payment; or

(B) on the filing of a complaint by the Secretary in an action under subsection (b) in which a recovery is sought of the damages described in paragraph (1)(A) owing to an eligible employee by an employer liable under paragraph (1), unless the action described in subparagraph (A) or (B) is dismissed without prejudice on motion of the Secretary.

(b) Action by the Secretary.—

(1) Administrative action.—The Secretary shall receive, investigate, and attempt to resolve complaints of violations of section 105 in the same manner that the Secretary receives, investigates, and attempts to resolve

complaints of violations of sections 6 and 7 of the Fair Labor Standards Act of 1938 (29 U.S.C. 206 and 207).

(2) Civil action.—The Secretary may bring an action in any court of competent jurisdiction to recover the damages described in subsection (a)(1)(A).

(3) Sums recovered.—Any sums recovered by the Secretary pursuant to paragraph (2) shall be held in a special deposit account and shall be paid, on order of the Secretary, directly to each employee affected. Any such sums not paid to an employee because of inability to do so within a period of 3 years shall be deposited into the Treasury of the United States as miscellaneous receipts.

(c) Limitation.—

(1) In general.—Except as provided in paragraph (2), an action may be brought under this section not later than 2 years after the date of the last event constituting the alleged violation for which the action is brought.

(2) Willful violation.—In the case of such action brought for a willful violation of section 105, such action may be brought within 3 years of the date of the last event constituting the alleged violation for which such action is brought.

(3) Commencement.—In determining when an action is commenced by the Secretary under this section for the purposes of this subsection, it shall be considered to be commenced on the date when the complaint is filed.

(d) Action for Injunction by Secretary.—The district courts of the United States shall have jurisdiction, for cause shown, in an action brought by the Secretary—

(1) to restrain violations of section 105, including the restraint of any withholding of payment of wages, salary, employment benefits, or other compensation, plus interest, found by the court to be due to eligible employees; or

(2) to award such other equitable relief as may be appropriate, including employment, reinstatement, and promotion.

(e) Solicitor of Labor.—The Solicitor of Labor may appear for and represent the Secretary on any litigation brought under this section.

SEC. 108. SPECIAL RULES CONCERNING EMPLOYEES OF LOCAL EDUCATIONAL AGENCIES.

(a) Application.—

(1) In general.—Except as otherwise provided in this section, the rights (including the rights under section 104, which shall extend throughout the period of leave of any employee under this section), remedies, and procedures under this title shall apply to—

(A) any "local educational agency" (as defined in section 1471(12) of the Elementary and Secondary Education Act of 1965 (20 U.S.C. 2891(12))) and an eligible employee of the agency; and

(B) any private elementary or secondary school and an eligible employee of the school.

(2) Definitions.—For purposes of the application described in paragraph (1):

(A) Eligible employee.—The term "eligible employee" means an eligible employee of an agency or school described in paragraph (1).

(B) Employer.—The term "employer" means an agency or school described in paragraph (1).

(b) Leave Does Not Violate Certain Other Federal Laws.—A local educational agency and a private elementary or secondary school shall not be in violation of the Individuals with Disabilities Education Act (20 U.S.C. 1400 et seq.), section 504 of the Rehabilitation Act of 1973 (29 U.S.C. 794), or title VI of the Civil Rights Act of 1964 (42 U.S.C. 2000d et seq.), solely as a result of an eligible employee of such agency or school exercising the rights of such employee under this title.

(c) Intermittent Leave or Leave on a Reduced Schedule for Instructional Employees.—

(1) In general.—Subject to paragraph (2), in any case in which an eligible employee employed principally in an instructional capacity by any such educational agency or school requests leave under subparagraph (C) or (D) section 102(a)(1) that is foreseeable based on planned medical treatment and the employee would be on leave for greater than 20 percent of the total number of working days in the period

during which the leave would extend, the agency or school may require that such employee elect either—

(A) to take leave for periods of a particular duration, not to exceed the duration of the planned medical treatment; or

(B) to transfer temporarily to an available alternative position offered by the employer for which the employee is qualified, and that—

(i) has equivalent pay and benefits; and

(ii) better accommodates recurring periods of leave than the regular employment position of the employee.

(2) Application.—The elections described in subparagraphs (A) and (B) of paragraph (1) shall apply only with respect to an eligible employee who complies with section 102(e)(2).

(d) Rules Applicable to Periods Near the Conclusion of an Academic Term.—The following rules shall apply with respect to periods of leave near the conclusion of an academic term in the case of any eligible employee employed principally in an instructional capacity by any such educational agency or school:

(1) Leave more than 5 weeks prior to end of term.—If the eligible employee begins leave under section 102 more than 5 weeks prior to the end of the academic term, the agency or school may require the employee to continue taking leave until the end of such term, if—

(A) the leave is of at least 3 weeks duration; and

(B) the return to employment would occur during the 3-week period before the end of such term.

(2) Leave less than 5 weeks prior to end of term.—If the eligible employee begins leave under subparagraph (A), (B), or (C) of section 102(a)(1) during the period that commences 5 weeks prior to the end of the academic term, the agency or school may require the employee to continue taking leave until the end of such term, if—

(A) the leave is of greater than 2 weeks duration; and

(B) the return to employment would occur during the 2-week period before the end of such term.

(3) Leave less than 3 weeks prior to end of term.—If the eligible employee begins leave under subparagraph (A), (B), or (C) of section 102(a)(1) during the period that commences 3 weeks prior to the end of the academic term and the duration of the leave is greater than 5 working days, the agency or school may require the employee to continue to take leave until the end of such term.

(e) Restoration of Equivalent Employment Position.—For purposes of determinations under section 104(a)(1)(B) (relating to the restoration of an eligible employee to an equivalent position), in the case of a local educational agency or a private elementary or secondary school, such determination shall be made on the basis of established school board policies and practices, private school policies and practices, and collective bargaining agreements.

(f) Reduction of the Amount of Liability.—If a local educational agency or a private elementary or secondary school that has violated this title proves to the satisfaction of the court that the agency, school, or department had reasonable grounds for believing that the underlying act or omission was not a violation of this title, such court may, in the discretion of the court, reduce the amount of the liability provided for under section 107(a)(1)(A) to the amount and interest determined under clauses (i) and (ii), respectively, of such section.

SEC. 109. NOTICE.

(a) In General.—Each employer shall post and keep posted, in conspicuous places on the premises of the employer where notices to employees and applicants for employment are customarily posted, a notice, to be prepared or approved by the Secretary, setting forth excerpts from, or summaries of, the pertinent provisions of this title and information pertaining to the filing of a charge.

(b) Penalty.—Any employer that willfully violates this section may be assessed a civil money penalty not to exceed $100 for each separate offense.

TITLE II—LEAVE FOR CIVIL SERVICE EMPLOYEES

SEC. 201. LEAVE REQUIREMENT.

(a) Civil Service Employees.—

(1) In general.—Chapter 63 of title 5, United States Code, is amended by adding at the end the following new subchapter:

"SUBCHAPTER V—FAMILY AND MEDICAL LEAVE

"Sec. 6381. Definitions

"For the purpose of this subchapter—

"(1) the term 'employee' means any individual who—

"(A) is an 'employee', as defined by section 6301(2), including any individual employed in a position referred to in clause (v) or (ix) of section 6301(2), but excluding any individual employed by the government of the District of Columbia and any individual employed on a temporary or intermittent basis; and

"(B) has completed at least 12 months of service as an employee (within the meaning of subparagraph (A));

"(2) the term 'health care provider' means—

"(A) a doctor of medicine or osteopathy who is authorized to practice medicine or surgery (as appropriate) by the State in which the doctor practices; and

"(B) any other person determined by the Director of the Office of Personnel Management to be capable of providing health care services;

"(3) the term 'parent' means the biological parent of an employee or an individual who stood in loco parentis to an employee when the employee was a son or daughter;

"(4) the term 'reduced leave schedule' means a leave schedule that reduces the usual number of hours per workweek, or hours per workday, of an employee;

"(5) the term 'serious health condition' means an illness, injury, impairment, or physical or mental condition that involves—

"(A) inpatient care in a hospital, hospice, or residential medical care facility; or

"(B) continuing treatment by a health care provider; and

"(6) the term 'son or daughter' means a biological, adopted, or foster child, a stepchild, a legal ward , or a child of a person standing in loco parentis, who is—

"(A) under 18 years of age; or

"(B) 18 years of age or older and incapable of self-care because of a mental or physical disability.

"Sec. 6382. Leave requirement

"(a)(1) Subject to section 6383, an employee shall be entitled to a total of 12 administrative workweeks of leave during any 12-month period for one or more of the following:

"(A) Because of the birth of a son or daughter of the employee and in order to care for such son or daughter.

"(B) Because of the placement of a son or daughter with the employee for adoption or foster care.

"(C) In order to care for the spouse, or a son, daughter, or parent, of the employee, if such spouse, son, daughter, or parent has a serious health condition.

"(D) Because of a serious health condition that makes the employee unable to perform the functions of the employee's position.

"(2) The entitlement to leave under subparagraph (A) or (B) of paragraph (1) based on the birth or placement of a son or daughter shall cxpirc at the end of the 12-month period beginning on the date of such birth or placement.

"(b)(1) Leave under subparagraph (A) or (B) of subsection (a)(1) shall not be taken by an employee intermittently or on a reduced leave schedule unless the employee and the employing agency of the employee agree otherwise. Subject to paragraph (2), subsection (e)(2), and section 6383(b)(5), leave under subparagraph (C) or (D) of subsection (a)(1) may be taken intermittently or on a reduced leave schedule when medically necessary. In the case of an employee who takes leave intermittently or on a reduced leave schedule pursuant to this paragraph, any hours of leave so taken by such employee shall be subtracted from the total amount of leave remaining available to such employee under subsection (a), for purposes of the 12-month period involved, on an hour-for-hour basis.

"(2) If an employee requests intermittent leave, or leave on a reduced leave schedule, under subparagraph (C) or (D) of subsection (a)(1), that is foreseeable based on planned medical treatment, the employing agency may require such employee to transfer temporarily to an available alternative position offered by the employing agency for which the employee is qualified and that—

"(A) has equivalent pay and benefits; and

"(B) better accommodates recurring periods of leave than the regular employment position of the employee.

"(c) Except as provided in subsection (d), leave granted under subsection (a) shall be leave without pay.

"(d) An employee may elect to substitute for leave under subparagraph (A), (B), (C), or (D) of subsection (a)(1) any of the employee's accrued or accumulated annual or sick leave under subchapter I for any part of the 12-week period of leave under such subsection, except that nothing in this subchapter shall require an employing agency to provide paid sick leave in any situation in which such employing agency would not normally provide any such paid leave.

"(e)(1) In any case in which the necessity for leave under subparagraph (A) or (B) of subsection (a)(1) is foreseeable based on an expected birth or placement, the employee shall provide the employing agency with not less than 30 days' notice, before the datc the leave is to begin, of the employee's intention to take leave under such subparagraph, except that if the date of the birth or placement requires leave to begin in less than 30 days, the employee shall provide such notice as is practicable.

"(2) In any case in which the necessity for leave under subparagraph (C) or (D) of subsection (a)(1) is foreseeable based on planned medical treatment, the employee—

"(A) shall make a reasonable effort to schedule the treatment so not to disrupt unduly the operations of the employing agency, subject to the approval of the health care provider of the employee or the health care provider of the son, daughter, spouse, or parent of the employee, as appropriate; and

"(B) shall provide the employing agency with not less than 30 days' notice, before the date the leave is to begin, of the employee's intention to take leave under such subparagraph, except that if the date of the treatment requires leave to begin in less than 30 days, the employee shall provide such notice as is practicable.

"Sec. 6383. Certification

"(a) An employing agency may require that a request for leave under subparagraph (C) or (D) of section 6382(a)(1) be supported by certification issued by the health care provider of the employee or of the son, daughter, spouse, or parent of the employee, as appropriate. The employee shall provide, in a timely manner, a copy of such certification to the employing agency.

"(b) A certification provided under subsection (a) shall be sufficient if it states—

"(1) the date on which the serious health condition commenced;

"(2) the probable duration of the condition;

"(3) the appropriate medical facts within the knowledge of the health care provider regarding the condition;

"(4)(A) for purposes of leave under section 6382(a)(1)(C), a statement that the employee is needed to care for the son, daughter, spouse, or parent, and an estimate of the amount of time that such employee is needed to care for such son, daughter, spouse, or parent; and

"(B) for purposes of leave under section 6382(a)(1)(D), a statement that the employee is unable to perform the functions of the position of the employee; and

"(5) in the case of certification for intermittent leave, or leave on a reduced leave schedule, for planned medical treatment, the dates on which such treatment is expected to be given and the duration of such treatment.

"(c)(1) In any case in which the employing agency has reason to doubt the validity of the certification provided under subsection (a) for leave under subparagraph (C) or (D) of section 6382(a)(1), the employing agency may require, at the expense of the agency, that the employee obtain the opinion of a second health care provider designated or approved by the employing agency concerning any information certified under subsection (b) for such leave.

"(2) Any health care provider designated or approved under paragraph (1) shall not be employed on a regular basis by the employing agency.

"(d)(1) In any case in which the second opinion described in subsection (c) differs from the original certification provided under subsection (a), the employing agency may require, at the expense of the agency, that the employee obtain the opinion of a third health care provider designated or approved jointly by the employing agency and the employee concerning the information certified under subsection (b).

"(2) The opinion of the third health care provider concerning the information certified under subsection (b) shall be considered to be final and shall be binding on the employing agency and the employee.

"(e) The employing agency may require, at the expense of the agency, that the employee obtain subsequent recertifications on a reasonable basis.

"Sec. 6384. Employment and benefits protection

"(a) Any employee who takes leave under section 6382 for the intended purpose of the leave shall be entitled, upon return from such leave—

"(1) to be restored by the employing agency to the position held by the employee when the leave commenced; or

"(2) to be restored to an equivalent position with equivalent benefits, pay, status, and other terms and conditions of employment.

"(b) The taking of leave under section 6382 shall not result in the loss of any employment benefit accrued prior to the date on which the leave commenced.

"(c) Except as otherwise provided by or under law, nothing in this section shall be construed to entitle any restored employee to—

"(1) the accrual of any employment benefits during any period of leave; or

"(2) any right, benefit, or position of employment, other than any right, benefit, or position to which the employee would have been entitled had the employee not taken the leave.

"(d) As a condition to restoration under subsection (a) for an employee who takes leave under section 6382(a)(1)(D), the employing agency may have a uniformly applied practice or policy that requires each such employee to receive certification from the health care provider of the employee that the employee is able to resume work.

"(e) Nothing in this section shall be construed to prohibit an employing agency from requiring an employee on leave under section 6382 to report periodically to the employing agency on the status and intention of the employee to return to work.

"Sec. 6385. Prohibition of coercion

"(a) An employee shall not directly or indirectly intimidate, threaten, or coerce, or attempt to intimidate, threaten, or coerce, any other employee for the purpose of interfering with the exercise of any rights which such other employee may have under this subchapter.

"(b) For the purpose of this section—

"(1) the term 'intimidate, threaten, or coerce' includes promising to confer or conferring any benefit (such as appointment, promotion, or compensation), or taking or threatening to take any reprisal (such as deprivation of appointment, promotion, or compensation); and

"(2) the term 'employee' means any 'employee', as defined by section 2105.

"Sec. 6386. Health insurance

"An employee enrolled in a health benefits plan under chapter 89 who is placed in a leave status under section 6382 may elect to continue the health benefits enrollment of the employee while in such leave status and arrange to pay currently into the Employees Health Benefits Fund (described in section 8909), the appropriate employee contributions.

"Sec. 6387. Regulations

"The Office of Personnel Management shall prescribe regulations necessary for the administration of this subchapter. The regulations prescribed under this subchapter shall, to the extent appropriate, be consistent with the regulations prescribed by the Secretary of Labor to carry out title I of the Family and Medical Leave Act of 1993."

(2) Table of contents.—The table of contents for chapter 63 of title 5, United States Code, is amended by adding at the end the following:

"SUBCHAPTER V—FAMILY AND MEDICAL LEAVE

"6381. Definitions.
"6382. Leave requirement.
"6383. Certification.
"6384. Employment and benefits protection.
"6385. Prohibition of coercion.
"6386. Health insurance.
"6387. Regulations.".

(b) Employees Paid From Nonappropriated Funds.—Section 2105(c)(1) of title 5, United States Code, is amended—

(1) by striking "or" at the end of subparagraph (C); and

(2) by adding at the end the following new subparagraph:

"(E) subchapter V of chapter 63, which shall be applied so as to construe references to benefit programs to refer to applicable programs for employees paid from nonappropriated funds; or".

TITLE III—COMMISSION ON LEAVE

SEC. 301. ESTABLISHMENT.

There is established a commission to be known as the Commission on Leave (referred to in this title as the "Commission").

SEC. 302. DUTIES.

The Commission shall—

(1) conduct a comprehensive study of—

(A) existing and proposed mandatory and voluntary policies relating to family and temporary medical leave, including policies provided by employers not covered under this Act;

(B) the potential costs, benefits, and impact on productivity, job creation and business growth of such policies on employers and employees;

(C) possible differences in costs, benefits, and impact on productivity, job creation and business growth of such policies on employers based on business type and size;

(D) the impact of family and medical leave policies on the availability of employee benefits provided by employers, including employers not covered under this Act;

(E) alternate and equivalent State enforcement of title I with respect to employees described in section 108(a);

(F) methods used by employers to reduce administrative costs of implementing family and medical leave policies;

(G) the ability of the employers to recover, under section 104(c)(2), the premiums described in such section; and

(H) the impact on employers and employees of policies that provide temporary wage replacement during periods of family and medical leave.

(2) not later than 2 years after the date on which the Commission first meets, prepare and submit, to the appropriate Committees of Congress, a report concerning the subjects listed in paragraph (1).

SEC. 303. MEMBERSHIP.

(a) Composition–

(1) Appointments.–The Commission shall be composed of 12 voting members and 4 ex officio members to be appointed not later than 60 days after the date of the enactment of this Act as follows:

(A) Senators.–One Senator shall be appointed by the Majority Leader of the Senate, and one Senator shall be appointed by the Minority Leader of the Senate.

(B) Members of house of representatives.–One Member of the House of Representatives shall be appointed by the Speaker of the House of Representatives, and one Member of the House of Representatives shall be appointed by the Minority Leader of the House of Representatives.

(C) Additional members.–

(i) Appointment.–Two members each shall be appointed by–

(I) the Speaker of the House of Representatives;

(II) the Majority Leader of the Senate;

(III) the Minority Leader of the House of Representatives; and

(IV) the Minority Leader of the Senate.

(ii) Expertise.—Such members shall be appointed by virtue of demonstrated expertise in relevant family, temporary disability, and labor management issues. Such members shall include representatives of employers, including employers from large businesses and from small businesses.

(2) Ex officio members.—The Secretary of Health and Human Services, the Secretary of Labor, the Secretary of Commerce, and the Administrator of the Small Business Administration shall serve on the Commission as nonvoting ex officio members.

(b) Vacancies.—Any vacancy on the Commission shall be filled in the manner in which the original appointment was made. The vacancy shall not affect the power of the remaining members to execute the duties of the Commission.

(c) Chairperson and Vice Chairperson.— The Commission shall elect a chairperson and a vice chairperson from among the members of the Commission.

(d) Quorum.—Eight members of the Commission shall constitute a quorum for all purposes, except that a lesser number may constitute a quorum for the purpose of holding hearings.

SEC. 304. COMPENSATION.

(a) Pay.—Members of the Commission shall serve without compensation.

(b) Travel Expenses.—Members of the Commission shall be allowed reasonable travel expenses, including a per diem allowance, in accordance with section 5703 of title 5, United States Code, when performing duties of the Commission.

SEC. 305. POWERS.

(a) Meetings.—The Commission shall first meet not later than 30 days after the date on which all members are appointed, and the Commission shall meet thereafter on the call of the chairperson or a majority of the members.

(b) Hearings and Sessions.—The Commission may hold such hearings, sit and act at such times and places, take such testimony, and receive such evidence as the Commission considers appropriate. The Commission may administer oaths or affirmations to witnesses appearing before it.

(c) Access to Information.—The Commission may secure directly from any Federal agency information necessary to enable it to carry out this title, if the information may be disclosed under section 552 of title 5, United States Code. Subject to the previous sentence, on the request of the chairperson or vice chairperson of the Commission, the head of such agency shall furnish such information to the Commission.

(d) Use of Facilities and Services.—Upon the request of the Commission, the head of any Federal agency may make available to the Commission any of the facilities and services of such agency.

(e) Personnel From Other Agencies.—On the request of the Commission, the head of any Federal agency may detail any of the personnel of such agency to serve as an Executive Director of the Commission or assist the Commission in carrying out the duties of the Commission. Any detail shall not interrupt or otherwise affect the civil service status or privileges of the Federal employee.

(f) Voluntary Service.—Notwithstanding section 1342 of title 31, United States Code, the chairperson of the Commission may accept for the Commission voluntary services provided by a member of the Commission.

SEC. 306. TERMINATION.

The Commission shall terminate 30 days after the date of the submission of the report of the Commission to Congress.

TITLE IV—MISCELLANEOUS PROVISIONS

SEC. 401. EFFECT ON OTHER LAWS.

(a) Federal and State Antidiscrimination Laws.—Nothing in this Act or any amendment made by this Act shall be construed to modify or affect any Federal or State law prohibiting discrimination on the basis of race, religion, color, national origin, sex, age, or disability.

(b) State and Local Laws.—Nothing in this Act or any amendment made by this Act shall be construed to supersede any provision of any State or local law that provides greater family or medical leave rights than the rights established under this Act or any amendment made by this Act.

SEC. 402. EFFECT ON EXISTING EMPLOYMENT BENEFITS.

(a) More Protective.—Nothing in this Act or any amendment made by this Act shall be construed to diminish the obligation of an employer to comply with any collective bargaining agreement or any employment benefit program or plan that provides greater family or medical leave rights to employees than the rights established under this Act or any amendment made by this Act.

(b) Less Protective.—The rights established for employees under this Act or any amendment made by this Act shall not be diminished by any collective bargaining agreement or any employment benefit program or plan.

SEC. 403. ENCOURAGEMENT OF MORE GENEROUS LEAVE POLICIES.

Nothing in this Act or any amendment made by this Act shall be construed to discourage employers from adopting or retaining leave policies more generous than any policies that comply with the requirements under this Act or any amendment made by this Act.

SEC. 404. REGULATIONS.

The Secretary of Labor shall prescribe such regulations as are necessary to carry out title I and this title not later than 120 days after the date of the enactment of this Act.

SEC. 405. EFFECTIVE DATES.

(a) Title III.—Title III shall take effect on the date of the enactment of this Act.

(b) Other Titles.—

(1) In general.—Except as provided in paragraph (2), titles I, II, and V and this title shall take effect 6 months after the date of the enactment of this Act.

(2) Collective bargaining agreements.—In the case of a collective bargaining agreement in effect on the effective date prescribed by paragraph (1), title I shall apply on the earlier of—

(A) the date of the termination of such agreement; or

(B) the date that occurs 12 months after the date of the enactment of this Act.

TITLE V—COVERAGE OF CONGRESSIONAL EMPLOYEES

SEC. 501. LEAVE FOR CERTAIN SENATE EMPLOYEES.

(a) Coverage.—The rights and protections established under sections 101 through 105 shall apply with respect to a Senate employee and an employing office. For purposes of such application, the term "eligible employee" means a Senate employee and the term "employer" means an employing office.

(b) Consideration of Allegations.—

(1) Applicable provisions.—The provisions of sections 304 through 313 of the Government Employee Rights Act of 1991 (2 U.S.C. 1204-1213) shall, except as provided in subsections (d) and (e)—

(A) apply with respect to an allegation of a violation of a provision of sections 101 through 105, with respect to Senate employment of a Senate employee; and

(B) apply to such an allegation in the same manner and to the same extent as such sections of the Government Employee Rights Act of 1991 apply with respect to an allegation of a violation under such Act.

(2) Entity.—Such an allegation shall be addressed by the Office of Senate Fair Employment Practices or such other entity as the Senate may designate.

(c) Rights of Employees.—The Office of Senate Fair Employment Practices shall ensure that Senate employees are informed of their rights under sections 101 through 105.

(d) Limitations.—A request for counseling under section 305 of such Act by a Senate employee alleging a violation of a provision of sections 101 through 105 shall be made not later than 2 years after the date of the last event constituting the alleged violation for which the counseling is requested, or not later than 3 years after such date in the case of a willful violation of section 105.

(e) Applicable Remedies.—The remedies applicable to individuals who demonstrate a violation of a provision of sections 101 through 105 shall be such remedies as would be appropriate if awarded under paragraph (1) or (3) of section 107(a).

(f) Exercise of Rulemaking Power.—The provisions of subsections (b), (c), (d), and (e), except as such subsections apply with respect to section 309 of the Government Employee Rights Act of 1991 (2 U.S.C. 1209), are enacted by the Senate as an exercise of the rulemaking power of the Senate, with full recognition of the right of the Senate to change its rules, in the same manner, and to the same extent, as in the case of any other rule of the Senate. No Senate employee may commence a judicial proceeding with respect to an allegation described in subsection (b)(1), except as provided in this section.

(g) Severability.—Notwithstanding any other provision of law, if any provision of section 309 of the Government Employee Rights Act of 1991 (2 U.S.C. 1209), or of subsection (b)(1) insofar as it applies such section 309 to an allegation described in subsection (b)(1)(A), is invalidated, both such section 309, and subsection (b)(1) insofar as it applies such section 309 to such an allegation, shall have no force and effect, and shall be considered to be invalidated for purposes of section 322 of such Act (2 U.S.C. 1221).

(h) Definitions.—As used in this section:

(1) Employing office.—The term "employing office" means the office with the final authority described in section 301(2) of such Act (2 U.S.C. 1201(2)).

(2) Senate employee.—The term "Senate employee" means an employee described in subparagraph (A) or (B) of section 301(c)(1) of such Act (2 U.S.C. 1201(c)(1)) who has been employed for at least 12 months on other than a temporary or intermittent basis by any employing office.

SEC. 502. LEAVE FOR CERTAIN HOUSE EMPLOYEES.

(a) In General.—The rights and protections under sections 102 through 105 (other than section 104(b)) shall apply to any employee in an employment position and any employing authority of the House of Representatives.

(b) Administration.—In the administration of this section, the remedies and procedures under the Fair Employment Practices Resolution shall be applied.

(c) Definition.—As used in this section, the term "Fair Employment Practices Resolution" means rule LI of the Rules of the House of Representatives.

TITLE VI—SENSE OF CONGRESS

SEC. 601. SENSE OF CONGRESS.

It is the sense of the Congress that:

(a) The Secretary of Defense shall conduct a comprehensive review of current departmental policy with respect to the service of homosexuals in the Armed Forces;

(b) Such review shall include the basis for the current policy of mandatory separation; the rights of all service men and women, and the effects of any change in such policy on morale, discipline, and military effectiveness.

(c) The Secretary shall report the results of such review and consultations and his recommendations to the President and to the Congress no later than July 15, 1993;

(d) The Senate Committee on Armed Services shall conduct (i) comprehensive hearings on the current military policy with respect to the service of homosexuals in the military services; and (ii) shall conduct oversight hearings on the Secretary's recommendations as such are reported.

Speaker of the House of Representatives.

Vice President of the United States and

President of the Senate.

§ 7.3 FMLA: Interim Regulations

Part 825—The Family and Medical Leave Act of 1993

Subpart A—What is the Family and Medical Leave Act, and to Whom Does It Apply?

825.113 What do "spouse," "parent," and "son or daughter" mean for purposes of an employee qualifying to take FMLA leave?

825.114 What is a "serious health condition"?

825.115 What does it mean that "the employee is unable to perform the functions of the position of the employee"?

825.116 What does it mean that an employee is "needed to care for" a family member?

825.117 For an employee seeking Intermittent FMLA leave or leave on a reduced leave schedule, what is meant by "the medical necessity for" such leave?

825.118 What is a "health care provider"?

Subpart B—What Leave Is an Employee Entitled To Take Under the Family and Medical Leave Act?

825.200 How much leave may an employee take?

825.201 If leave is taken for the birth of a child, or for placement of a child for adoption or foster care, when must the leave be concluded?

825.202 How much leave may a husband and wife take if they are employed by the same employer?

825.203 Does FMLA leave have to be taken all at once, or can it be taken in parts?

825.204 May an employer transfer an employee to an "alternative position" in order to accommodate intermittent leave or a reduced leave schedule?

825.205 How does one determine the amount of leave used where an employee takes leave intermittently or on a reduced leave schedule?

825.206 May an employer deduct hourly amounts from an employee's salary, when providing unpaid leave under FMLA, without affecting the employee's qualifications for exemption as an executive, administrative, or professional employee under the Fair Labor Standards Act?

825.207 Is FMLA leave paid or unpaid?

825.208 May an employer require an employee to designate paid leave as FMLA leave and, as a result, count it against the employee's total FMLA leave entitlement?

825.209 Is an employee entitled to benefits while using FMLA leave?

825.210 How may employees on FMLA leave pay their share of health benefit premiums?

825.211 What special health benefits maintenance rules apply to multi-employer health plans?

825.212 What are the consequences of an employee's failure to make timely health plan premium payments?

825.213 May an employer recover premiums it paid for maintaining "group health plan" coverage during FMLA leave?

825.214 What are an employee's rights on returning to work from FMLA leave?

825.215 What is an equivalent position?

825.216 Are there any limitations on an employer's obligation to reinstate an employee?

825.217 What is a "key employee"?

825.218 What does "substantial and grievous economic injury" mean?

825.219 What are the rights of a key employee?

825.220 How are employees who exercise their rights protected?

Subpart C—How Do Employees Learn of Their FMLA Rights and Obligations, and What Can an Employer Require of an Employee?

825.300 What posting requirements does the Act place on employers?

825.301 What other notices to employees are required of employer under the FMLA?

825.403 **How may an employer appeal the assessment of a penalty for willful violation of the posting requirement?**

825.404 **What are the consequences of an employer not paying the penalty assessment after a final order is issued?**

Subpart E—What Records Must Be Kept To Comply With the FMLA?

825.500 **What Records must an employer keep to comply with the FMLA?**

Subpart F—What Special Rules Apply to Employees of Schools?

825.600 **To whom do the special rules apply?**

825.601 **What limitations apply to the taking of intermittent leave or leave on a reduced leave schedule?**

825.602 **What limitations apply to the taking of leave near the end of an academic term?**

825.603 **Is all leave taken during "periods of a particular duration" counted against the FMLA leave entitlement?**

825.604 **What special rules apply to restoration to "an equivalent position?"**

Subpart G—How Do Other Laws, Employer Practices, and Collective Bargaining Agreements Affect Employee Rights Under FMLA?

825.700 **What if an employer provides more generous benefits than required by FMLA?**

825.701 **Do State laws providing family and medical leave still apply?**

825.702 **How does FMLA affect Federal and State anti-discrimination laws?**

Subpart H—Definitions

825.800 **Definitions**

Appendix A to Part 825—Index

Appendix B to Part 825—Certification of Physician or Practitioner

Appendix C to Part 825—Notice to Employees of Rights under FMLA

Authority: 29 U.S.C. 2654; Secretary's Order 1-93 (58 FR 21190).

Subpart A—What is the Family and Medical Leave Act, and to Whom Does It Apply?

§ 825.100 What is the Family and Medical Leave Act?

(a) The Family and Medical Leave Act of 1993 (FMLA or Act) gives "eligible" employees of a covered employer the right to take unpaid leave, or paid leave if it has been earned, for a period of up to 12 work-weeks in any 12 months because of the birth of a child or the placement of a child for adoption or foster care, because the employee is needed to care for a family member (child, spouse, or parent) with a serious health condition, or because the employee's own serious health condition makes the employee unable to do his or her job. Under certain circumstances, this leave may be taken on an intermittent basis rather than all at once, or the employee may work a part-time schedule.

(b) An employee on FMLA leave is also entitled to have health benefits maintained while on leave. If an employee was paying all or part of the premium payments prior to leave, the employee would continue to pay their share during the leave period. The employer can recover its share only if the employee dos not return to work for a reason other than the serious health condition of the employee or the employee's immediate family member, or another reason beyond the employee's control.

(c) An employee generally has a right to return to the same position or an equivalent position with equivalent pay, benefits and working conditions at the conclusion of the leave.

(d) The employer has a right to 30 days advance notice from the employee where practicable. In addition, the employer may require an employee to submit certification from a health care provider to substantiate that the leave is due to the serious health condition of the employee or the employee's immediate family member. Failure to comply with these requirements may result in the denial of FMLA leave. Pursuant to a uniformly applied policy, the employer may also require that an employee present a certification of fitness to return to work when the absence was caused by the employee's serious health condition. The employer may deny restoration to employment without such certificate relating to the health condition which caused the employee's absence.

§ 825.101 What is the purpose of the Act?

(a) FMLA is intended to allow employees to balance their work and family life by taking reasonable unpaid leave for medical reasons, for the birth or adoption of a child, and for the care of a child, spouse, or parent who has a serious health condition. The Act is intended to balance the demands of the workplace with the needs of families, to promote the stability and economic security of families, and to promote national interests in preserving family integrity. It was intended that the Act accomplish these purposes in a manner that accommodates the legitimate interests of employers, and in a manner consistent with the Equal Protection Clause of the Fourteenth Amendment in minimizing the potential for employment discrimination on the basis of sex, while promoting equal employment opportunity for men and women.

(b) The enactment of FMLA was predicated on two fundamental concerns—the needs of the American workforce, and the development of high-performance organizations. Increasingly, America's children and elderly are dependent upon family members who must spend long hours at work. When a family emergency arises, requiring workers to attend to seriously-ill children or parents, or to newly-born or adopted infants, or even to their own serious illness, workers need reassurance that they will not be asked to choose between continuing their employment, and meeting their personal and family obligations or tending to vital needs at home.

(c) The FMLA is both intended and expected to benefit employers as well as their employees. A direct correlation exists between stability in the family and productivity in the workplace. FMLA will encourage the development of high-performance organizations. When workers can count on durable links to their workplace they are able to make their own full commitments to their jobs. The record of hearings on family and medical leave indicate the powerful productive advantages of stable workplace relationships, and the comparatively small costs of guaranteeing that those relationships will not be dissolved while workers attend to pressing family health obligations or their own serious illness.

§ 825.102 When is the Act effective?

(a) The Act is effective on August 5, 1993. If a collective bargaining agreement is in effect on that date, the Act is effective on February 5,

1994, or the date the agreement expires, whichever is sooner. Application to collective bargaining agreements is discussed further in § 825.700(c).

(b) The period prior to the Act's effective date must be considered in determining employer coverage and employee eligibility. For example, as discussed further below, as of August 5, 1993, an employer must count employees/workweeks for calendar year 1992 and calendar year 1993 (to date). If 50 or more employees were employed during 20 or more workweeks in either 1992 or 1993 (year to date), the employer is covered under FMLA on August 5, 1993. If not, the employer is not covered on August 5, 1993, but must continue to monitor employment levels each workweek remaining in 1993 to determine if and when it might become covered.

§ 825.103 How does the Act affect leave in progress on, or taken before, the effective date of the Act?

(a) The right to take FMLA leave begins on the Act's effective date. Any leave taken prior to the Act's effective date may not be counted for purposes of FMLA. If leave qualifying as FMLA leave was underway prior to the effective date of the Act and continues after the Act's effective date, only that portion of leave taken on or after August 5, 1993, may be counted against the employee's leave entitlement under the FMLA.

(b) If an employer-approved leave is underway when the Act takes effect, no further notice may be required of the employee unless the employee requests an extension of the leave. For leave which commences on the effective date or shortly thereafter, such notice must be given which is practicable considering the foreseeability of the need for leave and the effective date of the statute.

(c) Starting on the Act's effective date, an employee is entitled to FMLA leave if the reason for the leave is qualifying under the Act, even if the event occasioning the need for leave (*e.g.,* the birth of a child) occurred before the effective date (so long as any other requirements are satisfied).

§ 825.104 What employers are covered by the Act?

(a) An employer covered by FMLA is any person engaged in commerce or in any industry or activity affecting commerce, who employs 50 or more employees for each working day during each of 20 or more calendar workweeks in the current or preceding calendar year. Employers covered by FMLA also include any person acting, directly or indirectly, in the interest of a covered employer to any of the employees of the employer, any successor in interest of a covered employer, and any public agency. Public agencies are covered employers without regard to the number of employees employed. Private elementary and secondary schools are also covered employers without regard to the number of employees employed. (See § 825.600.)

(b) The terms "commerce" and "industry affecting commerce" are defined in accordance with section 501(1) and (3) of the Labor Management Relations Act of 1947 (LMRA) (29 U.S.C. 142(1) and (3)), as set forth in the definitions at section 825.800 of this part. For purposes of the FMLA, employers who meet the 50-employee coverage test are deemed to be engaged in commerce or in an industry or activity affecting commerce.

(c) Normally the legal entity which employs the employee is the employer under FMLA. Applying this principle, a corporation is a single employer rather than its separate establishments or divisions.

(1) Where one corporation has an ownership interest in another corporation, it is a separate employer unless it meets the "joint employment" test discussed in § 825.106, or the "integrated employer" test contained in paragraph (c)(2) of this section.

(2) Separate entities will be deemed to be parts of a single employer for purposes of FMLA if they meet the "integrated employer" test. Where this test is met, the employees of all entities making up the integrated employer will be counted in determining employer coverage and employee eligibility. Factors considered in determining whether two or more entities are an integrated employer include:

(i) Common management;

(ii) Interrelation between operations;

(iii) Centralized control of labor relations; and

(iv) Degree of common ownership/financial control.

A determination of whether or not separate entities are an integrated employer is not determined by the application of any single criterion, but rather the entire relationship is to be reviewed in its totality.

(d) An "employer" includes any person who acts directly or indirectly in the interest of an employer to any of the employer's employees. The definition of "employer" in section 3(d) of the Fair Labor Standards Act (FLSA), 29 U.S.C. 203(d), similarly includes any person acting directly or indirectly in the interest of an employer in relation to an employee. As under the FLSA, individuals such as corporate officers "acting in the interest of an employer" are individually liable for any violations of the requirements of FMLA.

§ 825.105 In determining whether an employer is covered by FMLA, what does it mean to employ 50 or more employees for each working day during each of 20 or more calendar workweeks in the current or preceding calendar year?

(a) Any employee whose name appears on the employer's payroll will be considered employed each working day of the calendar week, and must be counted whether or not any compensation is received for the week.

(b) Employees on paid or unpaid leave, including FMLA leave, leaves of absence, disciplinary suspension, etc., are counted as long as the employer has a reasonable expectation that the employee will later return to active employment. Employees on layoff, whether temporary, indefinite or long-term, are not counted. Part-time employees, like full-time employees, are considered to be employed each working day of the calendar week, as long as they are maintained on the payroll.

(c) An employee who does not begin to work for an employer until after the first working day of a calendar week, or who terminates employment before the last working day of a calendar week, is not considered employed on each working day of that calendar week.

(d) A private employer is covered if it maintained 50 or more employees on the payroll during 20 or more calendar workweeks (not consecutive workweeks) in either the current or the preceding calendar year.

(e) Once a private employer meets the 50 employees/20 workweeks threshold, the employer remains covered until it reaches a future point where it no longer has employed 50 employees for 20 (nonconsecutive) workweeks in the current and preceding calendar year. For example, if an employer who meets the 50 employees/20 workweeks test in the current calendar year as of August 5, 1993, subsequently drops below 50 employees before the end of 1993 and continues to employ fewer than 50 employees in all workweeks throughout calendar year 1994, the employer continues to be covered throughout calendar year 1994 because it met the coverage criteria for 20 workweeks of the preceding (*i.e.,* 1993) calendar year.

§ 825.106 How is "joint employment" treated under FMLA?

(a) Where two or more businesses exercise some control over the work or working conditions of the employee, the businesses may be joint employers under FMLA. Joint employers may be separate and distinct entities with separate owners, managers and facilities. Factors which are considered in determining whether an employer-employee relationship exists include, but are not limited to:

(1) the nature and degree of control of the workers;

(2) The degree of supervision, direct or indirect, of the work;

(3) The power to determine the pay rates or the methods of payment of the workers;

(4) The right, directly or indirectly, to hire, fire, or modify the employment conditions of the workers; and

(5) Preparation of the payroll and payment of wages.

(b) A determination of whether or not a joint employment relationship exists is not determined by the application of any single criterion, but rather the entire relationship is to be viewed in its totality.

(c) A joint employment relationship often exists in situations:

(1) Where there is an arrangement between employers to share an employee's services or to interchange employees;

(2) Where one employer acts directly or indirectly in the interest of the other employer in relation to the employee; or,

(3) Where the employers are not completely disassociated with respect to the employee's employment and may be deemed to share control of the employee, directly or indirectly, because one employer controls, is controlled by, or is under common control with the other employer.

(d) Employees jointly employed by two employers must be counted by both employers, whether or not maintained on one of the employer's payroll, in determining employer coverage and employee eligibility. For example, an employer who jointly employs 15 workers from a leasing or temporary help agency and 40 permanent workers is covered by FMLA.

(e) In joint employment relationships, only the primary employer is responsible for giving required notices to its employees, providing leave, maintenance of health benefits, and job restoration. Factors considered in determining which is the "primary" employer include authority/responsibility to hire and fire, assign/place the employee, make the payroll, and provide employment benefits. For employees of temporary help or leasing agencies, for example, the placement agency most commonly would be the primary employer.

(f) A secondary employer with 50 or more employees—including jointly employed employees of *e.g.*, a temporary help agency—is responsible for compliance with the prohibited acts provisions (§ 825.220) with respect to its temporary/leased employees. These include prohibitions against interfering with an employee's attempt to exercise rights under the Act, or discharging or discriminating against an employee for opposing a practice which is unlawful under FMLA. The secondary employer will be responsible for compliance with all the provisions of the FMLA with respect to its regular, permanent workforce.

§ 825.107 What is meant by "successor in interest"?

(a) For purposes of FMLA, in determining whether an employer is covered because it is a "successor in interest" to a covered employer, the following factors will be considered:

(1) Substantial continuity of the same business operations;

(2) Use of the same plant;

(3) Continuity of the work force;

(4) Similarity of jobs and working conditions;

(5) Similarity of supervisory personnel;

(6) Similarity in machinery, equipment, and production methods;

(7) Similarity of products or services; and

(8) The ability of the predecessor to provide relief.

(b) A determination of whether or not a "successor in interest" exists is not determined by the application of any single criterion, but rather the entire circumstances are to be viewed in their totality.

(c) When an employer is a "successor in interest," employees' entitlements are the same as if the employment by the predecessor and successor were continuous employment by a single employer.

§ 825.108 What is a "public agency"?

(a) An "employer" under FMLA includes any "public agency," as defined in section 3(x) of the Fair Labor Standards Act, 29 U.S.C. 203(x). Section 3(x) of the FLSA defines "public agency" as the government of the United States; the government of a State or political subdivision of a State; or an agency of the United States, a State, or a political subdivision of a State, or any interstate governmental agency. "State" is further defined in Section 3(c) of the FLSA to include any State of the United States, the District of Columbia, or any Territory or possession of the United States.

(b) The determination of whether an entity is a "public" agency, as distinguished from a private employer, is determined by whether the agency has taxing authority, or whether the chief administrative officer or board, etc., is elected by the voters-at-large or their appointment is subject to approval by an elected official.

(c) A State or a political subdivision of a State constitutes a single public agency and, therefore, a single employer for purposes of determining employee eligibility. For example, a State is a single employer; a county is a single employer; a city or town is a single employer. Where there is any question about whether a public entity is a public agency, as distinguished form a part of another public agency, the U.S. Bureau of the Census' "Census of Governments" will be determinative, except for new entities formed since the most recent publication of the "Census." For new entities, the criteria used by the Bureau of Census will be used to determine whether an entity is a public agency or a part of another agency, including existence as an organized entity, governmental character, and substantial autonomy of the entity.

(d) All public agencies are covered by FMLA regardless of the number of employees; they are *not* subject to the coverage threshold of 50 employees carried on the payroll each day for 20 or more weeks in a year. However, employees of public agencies must meet all of the requirements of eligibility, including the requirement that the agency (*e.g.*, State) employ 50 employees at the worksite or within a 75-mile radius.

§ 825.109 Are Federal agencies covered by these regulations?

(a) Most employees of the government of the United States, if they are covered by the FMLA, are covered under Title II of the FMLA (incorporated in Title V, Chapter 63, Subchapter 5 of the United States Code) which is administered by the U.S. Office of Personnel Management (OPM). OPM has separate regulations at 5 CFR Part 630, Subpart L. In addition, employees of the Senate and House of Representatives are covered by Title V of the FMLA.

(b) The Federal Executive Branch employees within the jurisdiction of these regulations include:

(1) Employees of the Postal Service;

(2) Employees of the Postal Rate Commission;

(3) Employees of the Library of Congress;

(4) Employees of a corporation supervised by the Farm Credit Administration if private interests elect or appoint a member of the board of directors;

(5) A part-time employee who does not have an established regular tour of duty during the administrative workweek; and

(6) An employee serving under an intermittent appointment or temporary appointment with a time limitation of one year or less.

(c) Employees of other Federal executive agencies are also covered by these regulations if they are not covered by Title II of FMLA.

(d) Employees of the legislative or judicial branch of the United States are covered by these regulations only if they are employed in a unit which has employees in the competitive service. Examples include employees of the Government Printing Office and the U.S. Tax Court.

(e) For employees covered by these regulations, the U.S. Government constitutes a single employer for purposes of determining employee eligibility. These employees must meet all of the requirements for eligibility, including the requirement that the Federal Government employ 50 employees at the worksite or within a 75-mile radius.

§ 825.110 Which employees are "eligible" to take leave under FMLA?

(a) An "eligible employee" is an employee of a *covered* employer who:

(1) Has been employed by the employer for at least 12 months, and

(2) Has been employed for at least 1,250 hours of service during the 12-month period immediately preceding the commencement of the leave, and

(3) Is employed at a worksite where 50 or more employees are employed by the employer within 75 miles of that worksite.

(b) The 12 months an employee must have been employed by the employer need not be consecutive months. If an employee is maintained on the payroll for any part of a week, the week counts as a week of employment. For purposes of determining whether intermittent/occasional/casual employment qualifies as "at least 12 months," 52 weeks is deemed to be equal to 12 months.

(c) Whether an employee has worked the minimum 1,250 hours of service is determined according to the principles established under the Fair Labor Standards Act (FLSA) for determining compensable hours of work (*see* 29 CFR Part 785). The determining factor is the number of hours an employee has worked for the employer within the meaning of the FLSA. The determination is not limited by methods of recordkeeping, or by compensation agreements that do not accurately reflect all of the hours an employee has worked for or been in service to the employer. Any accurate accounting of actual hours worked under FLSA's principles may be used; in the absence of actual records of hours worked, employees who are exempt from FLSA's requirement that a record be kept of their hours worked (*e.g.*, bona fide executive, administrative, and professional employees as defined in FLSA Regulations, 29 CFR Part 541) and who have worked for the employer for at least 12 months will be presumed to have worked at least 1,250 hours during the previous 12 months. See § 825.500(d). For this purpose, full-time teachers (see § 825.800 for definition) of an elementary or secondary school system, or institution of higher education, or other educational establishment or institution are deemed to meet the 1,250 hour test. An employer must be able to clearly demonstrate that such an employee did not work 1,250 hours during the previous 12 months in order to claim that the employee is not "eligible" for FMLA leave.

(d) The determinations of whether an employee has worked for the employer for at least 1,250 hours in the past 12 months and has been employed by the employer for a total of at least 12 months must be made as of the date leave commences. If an employee notifies the employer of need for FMLA leave before the employee meets these eligibility criteria, the employer may confirm the employee's eligibility based upon a projection that the employee will be eligible on the date leave would commence or may advise the employee when the eligibility requirement is met. In the former case, the employer may not subsequently challenge the employee's eligibility and, provided the other requirements of these regulations are met, the employee will have satisfied the notice requirements even if not yet eligible for FMLA benefits.

(e) The period prior to the FMLA's effective date must be considered in determining employee's eligibility.

§ 825.111 In determining if an employee is "eligible" under FMLA, how is the determination made whether the employer employs 50 employees within 75 miles of the worksite where the employee requesting leave is employed?

(a) Generally, a worksite can refer to either a single location or a group of contiguous locations. Structures which form a campus or industrial park, or separate facilities in proximity with one another, may be considered a single site of employment. On the other hand, there may be several single sites of employment within a single building, such as an office building, if separate employers conduct activities within the building. For example, an office building with 50 different businesses as tenants will contain 50 sites of employment. The offices of each employer will be considered separate sites of employment for purposes of FMLA. An employee's worksite under FMLA will ordinarily be the site the employee reports to or, if none, from which the employee's work is assigned.

(1) Separate buildings or areas which are not directly connected or in immediate proximity are a single worksite if they are in reasonable geographic proximity, are used for the same purpose, and share the same staff and equipment. For example, if an employer manages a number of warehouses in a metropolitan area but regularly shifts or rotates the same employees from one building or another, the multiple warehouses would be a single worksite.

(2) For employees with no fixed worksite, *e.g.,* construction workers, transportation workers, salespersons, *etc.,* the "worksite" is the site to which they are assigned as their home base, from which their work is

assigned, or to which they report. For example, if a construction company headquartered in New Jersey opened a construction site in Ohio, and set up a mobile trailer on the construction site as the company's offices, the construction site in Ohio would be the worksite for any employees hired locally who report to the mobile trailer/company office daily for work assignments, *etc.* If that construction company also sent personnel such as job superintendents, foremen, engineers, an office manager, *etc.*, from New Jersey to the job site in Ohio, those workers sent from New Jersey continue to have the headquarters in New Jersey as their "worksite."

(b) The 75-mile radius is measured by road miles, using surface transportation over public streets, roads, highways and waterways, by the shortest route from the facility where the eligible employee requesting leave is employed.

(c) The determination of how many employees are employed within 75 miles of the worksite of an employee is based on the number of employees maintained on the payroll. Employees of educational institutions who are employed permanently or who are under contract are "maintained on the payroll" during any portion of the year when school is not in session.

(d) Whether 50 employees are employed within 75 miles to ascertain an employee's eligibility for FMLA benefits is determined when the employee requests the leave. Whether the leave is to be taken at one time or on an intermittent or reduced leave schedule basis, once an employee is determined eligible after requesting leave, the employee's eligibility is not affected by any subsequent change in the number of employees employed at or within 75 miles of the employee's worksite. Similarly, an employer may not terminate employee leave that has already started if the employee-count drops below 50. For example, if an employer employs 60 employees in August, but expects that the number of employees will drop to 40 in December, the employer must grant FMLA benefits to an employee who requests leave in August for a period of leave to begin in December.

§ 825.112 Under what kinds of circumstances are employers required to grant family or medical leave?

(a) Employers covered by FMLA are required to grant leave to eligible employees:

(1) For birth of a son or daughter, and to care for the newborn child;

(2) For placement with the employee of a son or daughter for adoption or foster care;

(3) To care for the employee's spouse, son, daughter, or parent with a serious health condition; and

(4) Because of a serious health condition that makes the employee unable to perform the functions of the employee's job.

(b) The right to take leave under FMLA applies equally to male and female employees. A father, as well as a mother, can take family leave for the birth, placement for adoption or foster care of a child.

(c) Circumstances may require that FMLA leave begin before the actual date of birth of a child. An expectant mother may take FMLA leave before the birth of the child for prenatal care or if her condition makes her unable to work.

(d) FMLA leave can being before the actual placement or adoption of a child if an absence from work is required for the placement for adoption or foster care to proceed. For example, the employee may be required to attend counselling sessions, appear in court, consult with his or her attorney or the doctor(s) representing the birth parent, or submit to a physical examination. The source of an adopted child (*e.g.,* whether from a licensed placement agency or otherwise) is not a factor in determining eligibility for leave for this purpose. There is no maximum age limit on a child being adopted or placed for foster care for purposes of determining eligibility for leave.

(e) Foster care is 24-hour care for children in substitution for, and away from, their parents or guardian. Such placement is made by or with the agreement of the State as a result of a voluntary agreement between the parent or guardian that the child be removed from the home, or pursuant to a judicial determination of the necessity for foster care, and involves agreement between the State and foster family that the foster family will take care of the child. Although foster care may be with relatives of the child, State action is involved in the removal of the child from parental custody.

§ 825.113 What do "spouse," "parent," and "son or daughter" mean for purposes of an employee qualifying to take FMLA leave?

(a) Spouse means a husband or wife as defined or recognized under State law for purposes of marriage, including common law marriage in States where it is recognized.

(b) Parent means a biological parent or an individual who stands or stood *in loco parentis* to an employee when the employee was a child. This term does not include parents "in law."

(c) Son or daughter means a biological, adopted, or foster child, a stepchild, a legal ward, or a child of a person standing *in loco parentis,* who is either under age 18, or age 18 or older and "incapable of self-care because of a mental or physical disability."

(1) "Incapable of self-care" means that the individual requires active assistance or supervision to provide daily self-care in several of the "activities of daily living" or "ADLs." Activities of daily living include adaptive activities such as caring appropriately for one's grooming and hygiene, bathing, dressing, eating, cooking, cleaning, shopping, taking public transportation, paying bills, maintaining a residence, using telephones and directories, using a post office, etc.

(2) "Physical or mental disability" means a physical or mental impairment that substantially limits one or more of the major life activities of an individual. Regulations at 29 CFR Part 1630, issued by the Equal Employment Opportunity Commission under the Americans with Disabilities Act (ADA), 42 U.S.C. 12101 *et seq.,* define these terms.

(3) Persons who are "*in loco parentis*" include those with day-to-day responsibilities to care for and financially support a child or, in the case of an employee, who had such responsibility for the employee when the employee was a child. A biological or legal relationship is not necessary.

§ 825.114 What is a "serious health condition"?

(a) For purposes of FMLA, "serious health condition" means an illness, injury, impairment, or physical or mental condition that involves:

(1) Any period of incapacity or treatment in connection with or consequent to inpatient care (*i.e.,* an overnight stay) in a hospital, hospice, or residential medical care facility;

(2) Any period of incapacity requiring absence from work, school, or other regular daily activities, of more than three calendar days, that also involves continuing treatment by (or under the supervision of) a health care provider; or

(3) Continuing treatment by (or under the supervision of) a health care provider for a chronic or long-term health condition that is incurable

or so serious that, if not treated, would likely result in a period of incapacity of more than three calendar days; or for prenatal care.

(b) "Continuing treatment by a health care provider" means one or more of the following:

(1) The employee or family member in question is treated two or more times for the injury or illness by a health care provider. Normally this would require visits to the health care provider or to a nurse or physician's assistant under direct supervision of the health care provider.

(2) The employee or family member is treated for the injury or illness two or more times by a provider of health care services (*e.g.,* physical therapist) under orders of, or on referral by, a health care provider, *or* is treated for the injury or illness by a health care provider on at least one occasion which results in a regimen of continuing treatment under the supervision of the health care provider—for example, a course of medication or therapy—to resolve the health condition.

(3) The employee or family member is under the continuing supervision of, but not necessarily being actively treated by, a health care provider due to a serious long-term or chronic condition or disability which cannot be cured. Examples include persons with Alzheimer's, persons who have suffered a severe stroke, or persons in the terminal stages of a disease who may not be receiving active medical treatment.

(c) Voluntary or cosmetic treatments (such as most treatments for orthodontia or acne) which are not medically necessary are not "serious health conditions," unless inpatient hospital care is required. Restorative dental surgery after an accident, or removal of cancerous growths are serious health conditions provided all the other conditions of this regulation are met. Treatments for allergies or stress, or for substance abuse, are serious health conditions if all the conditions of the regulation are met. Prenatal care is included as a serious health condition. Routine preventive physical examinations are excluded.

(d) The scope of "serious health condition" is further clarified by the requirements of the Act that the health care provider may be required to certify; in the case of family medical leave, that the "employee is needed to care for" the family member; in the case of medical leave, that "the employee is unable to perform the functions of the position of the employee"; and, in addition, in the case of leave taken "intermittently or on a reduced leave schedule," the medical necessity for such leave. (See §§ 825.115, 825.116, 825.117, 825.306, 825.310, and 825.311.)

§ 825.115 What does it mean that "the employee is unable to perform the functions of the position of the employee"?

An employee is "unable to perform the functions of the position" where the health care provider finds that the employee is unable to work at all or is unable to perform any of the essential functions of the employee's position within the meaning of the Americans with Disabilities Act (ADA), 42 USC 12101 *et seq.*, and the regulations at 29 CFR Part 1630. An employer has the option, in requiring certification from a health care provider, to provide a statement of the essential functions of the employee's position for the provider to review.

§ 825.116 What does it mean that an employee is "needed to care for" a family member?

(a) The medical certification provision that an employee is "needed to care for" a family member encompasses both physical and psychological care. It includes situations where, for example, because of a serious health condition, the family member is unable to care for his or her own basic medical, hygienic, or nutritional needs or safety, or is unable to transport himself or herself to the doctor, etc. The term also includes providing psychological comfort and reassurance which would be a beneficial to a seriously ill child or parent receiving inpatient care.

(b) The term also includes situations where the employee may be needed to fill in for others who are caring for the family member, or to make arrangements for changes in care, such as transfer to a nursing home.

(c) An employee's intermittent leave or a reduced leave schedule necessary to care for a family member includes not only a situation where the family member's condition itself is intermittent, but also where the employee is only needed intermittently—such as where other care is normally available, or care responsibilities are shared with another member of the family or a third party.

§ 825.117 For an employee seeking intermittent FMLA leave or leave on a reduced leave schedule, what is meant by "the medical necessity for" such leave?

For intermittent leave or leave on a reduced leave schedule, there must be a medical need for leave (as distinguished from voluntary treatments and procedures) and it must be that such medical need can be best accommodated through an intermittent or reduced leave schedule. The treatment regimen and other information described in the certification of a serious health condition (*see* § 825.306) meets the requirement for certification of the medical necessity of intermittent leave or leave on a reduced leave schedule. Employees needing intermittent FMLA leave or leave on a reduced leave schedule must attempt to schedule their leave so as not to disrupt the employer's operations. In addition, an employer may assign an employee to an alternative position with equivalent pay and benefits that better accommodates the employee's intermittent or reduced leave schedule.

§ 825.118 What is a "health care provider"?

(a) The Act defines "health care provider" as:

(1) A doctor of medicine or osteopathy who is authorized to practice medicine or surgery (as appropriate) by the State in which the doctor practices; or

(2) Any other person determined by the Secretary to be capable of providing health care services.

(b) Others "capable of providing health care services" include only:

(1) Podiatrists, dentists, clinical psychologists, optometrists, and chiropractors (limited to treatment consisting of manual manipulation of the spine to correct a subluxation as demonstrated by X-ray to exist) authorized to practice in the State and performing within the scope of their practice as defined under State law;

(2) Nurse practitioners and nurse-midwives who are authorized to practice under State law and who are performing within the scope of their practice as defined under State law; and

(3) Christian Science practitioners listed with the First Church of Christ, Scientist in Boston, Massachusetts. Where an employee or family member is receiving treatment from a Christian Science practitioner, an employee may not object to any requirement from an employer that the employee or family member submit to examination (though not treatment) to obtain a second or third certification from a health care provider other than a Christian Science practitioner.

Subpart B—What Leave Is an Employee Entitled to take under the Family and Medical Leave Act?

§ 825.200 How much leave may an employee take?

(a) An eligible employee is entitled to a total of 12 workweeks of leave during any 12-month period for any one, or more, of the following reasons:

(1) The birth of a son or daughter, and to care for the newborn child;

(2) The placement with the employee of a son or daughter for adoption or foster care;

(3) To care for the employee's spouse, son, daughter, or parent with a serious health condition; and,

(4) Because of a serious health condition that makes the employee unable to perform the functions of his or her job.

(b) An employer is permitted to choose any one of the following methods for determining the "12-month period" in which the 12 weeks of leave entitlement occurs:

(1) The calendar year;

(2) Any fixed 12-month "leave year," such as a fiscal year, a year required by State law, or a year starting on an employee's "anniversary" date;

(3) The 12-month period measured forward from the date any employee's first FMLA leave begins; or,

(4) A "rolling" 12-month period measured backward from the date an employee uses any FMLA leave (except that such measure may not extend back before August 5, 1993).

(c) Under methods in paragraphs (b)(1) and (b)(2) of this section an employee would be entitled to up to 12 weeks of FMLA leave at any time in the fixed 12-month period selected. An employee could, therefore, take 12 weeks of leave at the end of the year and 12 weeks at the beginning of the following year. Under the method in paragraph (b)(3) of this section, an employee would be entitled to 12 weeks of leave during the year beginning on the first date FMLA leave is taken; the next 12-month period would begin the first time FMLA leave is taken after completion of any previous 12-month period. Under the method in paragraph (b)(4) of this section, the "rolling" 12-month period, each time an employee takes FMLA leave the remaining leave entitlement would be any balance of the 12 weeks which has not been used during the immediately preceding 12 months. For example, if an employee has taken eight weeks of leave during the past 12 months, an additional four weeks of leave could be taken. If an employee used four weeks beginning February 1, 1994, four weeks beginning June 1, 1994, and four weeks beginning December 1, 1994, the employee would not be entitled to any additional leave until February 1, 1995. However, on February 1, 1995, the employee would be entitled to four weeks of leave, on June 1 the employee would be entitled to an additional four weeks, *etc.*

(d) Employers will be allowed to choose any one of the alternatives in paragraph (b) of this section provided the alternative chosen is applied consistently and uniformly to all employees. An employer wishing to change to another alternative is required to give at least 60 days notice to all employees, and the transition must take place in such a way that the employees retain the full benefit of 12 weeks of leave under whichever method affords the greatest benefit to the employee. Under no circumstances may a new method be implemented in order to avoid the Act's leave requirements.

(e) Methods for determining an employee's 12-week leave entitlement are described in § 825.205.

§ 825.201 If leave is taken for the birth of a child, or for placement of a child for adoption or foster care, when must the leave be concluded?

An employee's entitlement to leave for a birth or placement for adoption or foster care expires at the end of the 12-month period beginning on the date of the birth or placement, unless state law allows, or the employer permits, leave to be taken for a longer period. Any such FMLA leave must be concluded within this one-year period.

§ 825.202 How much leave may a husband and wife take if they are employed by the same employer?

(a) A husband and wife who are eligible for FMLA leave and are employed by the same covered employer are permitted to take only a combined total of 12 weeks of leave during any 12-month period if the leave is taken:

(1) for birth of a son or daughter or to care for the child after birth;

(2) for placement of a son or daughter for adoption or foster care, or to care for the child after placement; or

(3) to care for a parent (but not a parent "in-law") with a serious health condition.

(b) This limitation on the total weeks of leave applies as long as a husband and wife are employed by the "same employer." It would apply, for example, even though the spouses are employed at two different worksites of an employer located more than 75 miles from each other, or by two different operating divisions of the same company. On the other hand, if one spouse is ineligible for FMLA leave, the other spouse would be entitled to a full 12 weeks of FMLA leave.

(c) Where the husband and wife both use a portion of the total 12-week FMLA leave entitlement for one of the purposes in paragraph (a) of this section, the husband and wife would each be entitled to the difference between the amount he or she has taken individually and 12 weeks for FMLA leave for a purpose other than those contained in paragraph (a) of this section. For example, if each spouse took 6 weeks of leave for the birth of a child, each could later use an additional 6 weeks due to a personal illness or to take care of a sick child.

§ 825.203 Does FMLA leave have to be taken all at once, or can it be taken in parts?

(a) FMLA leave may be taken "intermittently or on a reduced leave schedule" under certain circumstances. Where leave is taken because of a birth or placement of a child for adoption or foster care, an employee may take leave intermittently or on a reduced leave schedule only if the employer agrees. Where FMLA leave is taken to care for a sick family member or for an employee's own serious health condition, leave may be taken intermittently or on a reduced leave schedule when medically necessary.

(b) "Intermittent leave" is leave taken in separate blocks of time due to a single illness or injury, rather than for one continuous period of time, and may include leave of periods from an hour or more to several weeks. Examples of intermittent leave would include leave taken on an occasional basis for medical appointments, or leave taken several days at a time spread over a period of six months, such as for chemotherapy.

(c) A "reduced leave schedule" is a leave schedule that reduces an employee's usual number of working hours per workweek, or hours per workday. In other words, a reduced leave schedule is a change in the employee's schedule for a period of time, normally from full-time to part-time. Such a schedule reduction might occur, for example, where an employee, with the employer's agreement, works part-time after the birth of a child; or because an employee who is recovering from a serious health condition is not strong enough to work a full-time schedule.

(d) There is no limit on the size of an increment of leave when an employee takes intermittent leave or leave on a reduced leave schedule. However, an employer may limit leave increments to the shortest period of time (one hour or less) that the employer's payroll system uses to account for absences or use of leave. For example, an employee might take two hours off for a medical appointment, or might work a reduced day of four hours over a period of several weeks while recuperating from an illness.

§ 825.204 May an employer transfer an employee to an "alternative position" in order to accommodate intermittent leave or a reduced leave schedule?

(a) If an employee requests intermittent leave or leave on a reduced leave schedule that is foreseeable based on planned medical treatment, including during a period of recovery from a serious health condition, the employer may require the employee to transfer temporarily to an available alternative position for which the employee is qualified and which better accommodates recurring periods of leave than does the employee's regular position.

(b) Transfer to an alternative position may require compliance with any applicable collective bargaining agreement, federal law (such as the Americans with Disabilities Act), and State law. Transfer to an alternative position may include altering an existing job to better accommodate the employee's need for intermittent or reduced leave.

(c) The alternative position must have equivalent pay and benefits. An alternative position for these purposes does not have to have equivalent duties. The employer may increase the pay and benefits of an existing alternative position, so as to make them equivalent to the employee's regular job. The employer may also transfer the employee to a part-time job with the same hourly rate of pay and benefits, provided the employee is not required to take more leave than is medically necessary. For example, an employee desiring to take leave in increments of 4 hours per day could be transferred to a half-time job paying the same hourly rate as the employee's previous job and enjoying the same benefits. The employer may not eliminate benefits which otherwise would not be provided to part-time employees; however, an employer may proportionately reduce earned benefits, such as vacation leave, where such a reduction is normally made by an employer for its part-time employees.

§ 825.205 How does one determine the amount of leave used where an employee takes leave intermittently or on a reduced leave schedule?

(a) If an employee takes leave on an intermittent or reduced leave schedule, only the amount of leave actually taken may be counted toward the 12 weeks of leave to which an employee is entitled. For example, if an employee who normally works five days a week takes off one day, the employee would use 1/5 of a week of FMLA leave. Similarly, if a full-time employee who normally works 8-hour days works 4-hour days under a reduced leave schedule, the employee would use 1/2 week of FMLA leave each week.

(b) Where an employee normally works a part-time schedule or variable hours, the amount of leave to which an employee is entitled is determined on a pro rata or proportional basis by comparing the new schedule with the employee's normal schedule. For example, if an employee who normally works 30 hours per week works only 20 hours a week under a reduced leave schedule, the employee's ten hours of leave would constitute one-third of a week of FMLA leave for each week the employee works the reduced leave schedule.

(c) If an employer has made a permanent or long-term change in the employee's schedule (for reasons other than FMLA), the hours worked under the new schedule are to be used for making this calculation.

(d) If an employee's schedule varies from week to week, a weekly average of the hours worked over the 12 weeks prior to the beginning of the leave period would be used for calculating the employee's normal workweek.

§ 825.206 May an employer deduct hourly amounts from an employee's salary, when providing unpaid leave under FMLA, without affecting the employee's qualification for exemption as an executive, administrative, or professional employee under the Fair Labor Standards Act?

(a) Leave taken under FMLA may be unpaid. If an employee is otherwise exempt from minimum wage and overtime requirements of the Fair Labor Standards Act (FLSA) as a salaried executive, administrative, or professional employee (under regulations issued by the Secretary), 29 CFR Part 541, providing unpaid FMLA-required leave to such an employee will not cause the employee to lose the FLSA exemption. This means that under regulations currently in effect, where an employee meets the specified duties test, and is paid, on a salary basis, a salary of at least the amount specified in the regulations, the employer may make deductions from the employee's salary for any hours taken as intermittent or reduced FMLA leave within a workweek, without affecting the exempt status of the employee. The fact that an employer provides FMLA leave, whether paid or unpaid, and maintains records required by this part regarding FMLA leave, will not be relevant to the determination whether an employee is exempt within the meaning of 29 CFR Part 541.

(b) This special exception to the "salary basis" requirements of the FLSA exemption applies only to employees of covered employers who are eligible for FMLA leave, and to leave which qualifies as (one of the four types of) FMLA leave. Hourly or other deductions which are not in accordance with 29 CFR Part 541 may *not* be taken for example, from the salary of an otherwise exempt employee who works for an employer with fewer than 50 employees, or where the employee has not worked long enough to be eligible for FMLA leave without potentially affecting the employee's eligibility for exemption. Nor may deductions which are not permitted by Part 541 be taken from such an employee's salary for any leave which does not qualify as FMLA leave, for example, deductions from an employee's pay for leave required under State law or under an employer's policy or practice for a reason which does not qualify as FMLA leave, *e.g.,* leave to care for a grandparent or for a medical condition which does not qualify as a serious health condition; or for leave which is more generous than provided by FMLA, such as leave in excess of 12 weeks in a year. Employers may comply with State law or thc cmployer's own policy/practice under these circumstances and maintain the employee's eligibility for exemption by not taking hourly deductions from the employee's pay, in accordance with FLSA requirements, or may take such deductions, treating the employee as an "hourly" employee and pay overtime premium pay for hours worked over 40 in a workweek.

§ 825.207 Is FMLA leave paid or unpaid?

(a) Generally, FMLA leave is unpaid. However, under the circumstances described in this section, FMLA permits an eligible employee to choose to substitute paid leave for FMLA leave, and an employer to require an employee to substitute paid leave for FMLA leave.

(b) Where an employee has earned or accrued paid vacation, personal or family leave, that leave may be substituted for all or part of any (otherwise) unpaid FMLA leave relating to birth, placement of a child for adoption or foster care, or care for a family member. An employee is entitled to substitute paid family leave only under circumstances permitted by the employer's family leave plan. For example, if the employer's leave plan allows use of family leave to care for a child but not for parent, the employer may but is not required to allow accrued family leave to be substituted for FMLA leave used to care for a parent.

(c) Substitution of paid accrued vacation, personal, or medical/sick leave may be made for all or part of any (otherwise) unpaid FMLA leave needed to care for a family member or the employee's own serious health condition. However, an employer may but is *not* required to, allow substitution of paid sick or medical leave for unpaid FMLA leave "in any situation" where the employer would not normally allow such paid leave.

(1) An employee has a right to substitute paid medical/sick leave to care for a seriously ill family member only if the employer's leave plan allows paid leave to be used for that purpose. Similarly, an employee does not have a right to substitute paid medical/sick leave for a serious health condition which is not covered by the employer's leave plan.

(2) Paid leave provided under a plan covering temporary disabilities is considered sick/medical leave for purposes of FMLA substitution. For example disability leave for the birth of a child would be considered FMLA leave for a serious health condition and counted in the 12 weeks of leave permitted under FMLA.

(d) Paid vacation or personal leave, including leave earned or accrued under plans allowing "paid time off," may be substituted, at either the employee's or the employer's option, for any qualified FMLA leave. No limitations may be placed by the employer on substitution of paid vacation or personal leave for these purposes.

(e) If neither the employee nor the employer elects to substitute paid leave for unpaid FMLA leave under the above conditions and circumstances, the employee will remain entitled to all the paid leave which is earned or accrued under the terms of the employer's plan.

(f) If an employee uses paid leave under circumstances which do not qualify as FMLA leave, the leave will not count against the 12 weeks of FMLA leave to which the employee is entitled. For example, paid sick leave used for a medical condition which is not a serious health condition does not count against the 12 weeks of FMLA leave entitlement.

(g) Whenever an employee uses paid leave, the employee can only be required to comply with the requirements of the employer's leave plan, and not any more stringent requirements of FMLA (*e.g.*, notice or certification requirements) unless the paid leave period is followed by a period of unpaid FMLA leave. For example, an employee having only four weeks of sick leave available under the employer's plan, may need to take an additional four weeks of unpaid FMLA leave. If the employee requests a total of eight weeks of leave, FMLA notice and certification may be required by the employer (unless such notice and certification would not otherwise be required by the employer of employees using unpaid leave for such a period of time).

§ 825.208 May an employer require an employee to designate paid leave as FMLA leave and, as a result, count it against the employee's total FMLA leave entitlement?

(a) An employee requesting unpaid FMLA leave must explain the reasons for the needed leave so as to allow the employer to determine that the leave qualifies under the Act. In many cases, in explaining the reasons for a request to use paid leave, especially when the need for the leave was unexpected or unforeseen, an employee will (even though, under the employer's policy, they may not be required to) provide sufficient information for the employer to designate the paid leave as substituting for all or some portion of the employee's FMLA leave entitlement. An employee using accrued paid leave, especially vacation or personal leave, may in some cases not spontaneously explain the reasons or their plans for using their accrued leave.

(1) As noted in § 825.302(c), an employee giving notice of the need for unpaid FMLA leave does not need to expressly assert rights under the Act or even mention the FMLA to meet their obligation to provide notice, though they would need to state a qualifying reason for the needed leave. An employee requesting or notifying the employer of an intent to use accrued paid leave, even if for a purpose covered by FMLA, would not need to assert such right either. However, if an employee requesting to use paid leave for an FMLA-qualifying purpose does not explain the reason for the leave—consistent with the employer's established policy or practice—and the employer denies the employee's request, the employee will need to provide sufficient information to establish an FMLA-qualifying reason for the needed leave so that the employer is aware of the

employee's entitlement (i.e., that the leave may not be denied) and, then, may designate that the paid leave be appropriately counted against (substituted for) the employee's 12-week entitlement. Similarly, an employee using accrued paid vacation leave who seeks an extension of unpaid leave for an FMLA-qualifying purpose will need to state the reason. If this is due to an event which occurred during the period of paid leave, the employer may count the leave used after the FMLA-qualifying event against the employee's 12-week entitlement.

(2) In all circumstances, it is the employer's responsibility to designate leave, paid or unpaid, as FMLA-qualifying, based on information provided by the employee. In any circumstance where the employer does not have sufficient information about the reason for an employee's use of paid leave, the employer should inquire further to ascertain whether the paid leave is potentially FMLA-qualifying.

(b) The employer may designate paid leave as FMLA leave only on the basis of information provided by the employee to the employer (as opposed to information sought or obtained from another party). The employer must immediately notify the employee that the paid leave is designated (see § 825.301(c)), and will be counted as FMLA leave. If there is a dispute between an employer and an employee as to whether paid leave qualifies as FMLA leave, it should be resolved through discussions between the employee and the employer.

(c) If the employer requires paid leave to be substituted for unpaid leave, or that paid leave taken under an existing leave plan be counted as FMLA leave, this decision must be made by the employer at the time the employee requests or gives notice of the leave, or when the employer determines that the leave qualifies as FMLA leave if this happens later. The employer's designation must be made before the leave starts, or before an extension of the leave is granted, unless the employer does not have sufficient information as to the employee's reason for taking the leave until after the leave commenced. In no event may an employer designate leave as FMLA leave after the leave has ended.

(d) If either the employer or the employee designates leave as FMLA leave after leave has begun, such as when an employer requests an extension of the paid leave with unpaid FMLA leave, the entire or some portion of the paid leave period may be retroactively counted as FMLA leave, to the extent that the leave period qualified as FMLA leave.

§ 825.209 Is an employee entitled to benefits while using FMLA leave?

(a) During any FMLA leave, an employer must maintain the employee's coverage under any group health plan (as defined in the Internal Revenue Code of 1986 at 26 U.S.C. 5000(b)(1)) on the same conditions as coverage would have been provided if the employee had been continuously employed during the entire leave period. All employers covered by FMLA, including public agencies, are subject to the Act's requirements to maintain health coverage. The definition of "group health plan" is set forth in § 825.800.

(b) The same health benefits provided to an employee prior to taking FMLA leave must be maintained during the FMLA leave. For example, if family member coverage is provided to an employee, family member coverage must be maintained during the FMLA leave. Similarly, benefit coverage during FMLA leave for medical care, surgical care, hospital care, dental care, eye care, mental health counseling, substance abuse treatment, *etc.,* must be maintained during leave if provided in an employer's group health plan, including a supplement to a group health plan, whether or not provided through a flexible spending account or other component of a cafeteria plan.

(c) If an employer provides a new health plan or benefits or changes health benefits or plans while an employee is on FMLA leave, the employee is entitled to the new or changed plan/benefits to the same extent as if the employee were not on leave. For example, if an employer changes a group health plan so that dental care becomes covered under the plan, an employee on FMLA leave must be given the same opportunity as other employees to receive (or obtain) the dental care coverage.

(d) Notice of any opportunity to change plans or benefits must also be given to an employee on FMLA leave. If the plan permits an employee to change from single to family coverage upon the birth of a child or otherwise add new family members, such a change in benefits must be made available while an employee is on FMLA leave. If the employee requests the changed coverage it must be provided by the employer.

(e) An employee may choose not to retain health coverage during FMLA leave. However, when an employee returns from leave, the employee is entitled to be reinstated on the same terms as prior to taking the leave, without any qualifying period, physical examination, exclusion of pre-existing conditions, *etc.*

(f) Except as required by the Consolidated Omnibus Budget Reconciliation Act of 1986 (COBRA) and for "key" employees (as discussed below), an employer's obligation to maintain health benefits under FMLA ceases if and when an employee informs the employer of his or her intent not to return from leave (including at the start of leave if the employer is so informed before the leave starts), or the employee fails to return from leave, and thereby terminates employment, or the employee exhausts his or her FMLA leave entitlement.

(g) If a "key employee" (see § 825.218) does not return from leave when notified by the employer that substantial or grievous economic injury will result from his or her reinstatement, the employee's entitlement to group health benefits continues unless and until the employee advises the employer that the employee does not desire restoration to employment at the end of the leave period, or FMLA leave entitlement is exhausted, or reinstatement is actually denied.

§ 825.210 How many employees on FMLA leave pay their share of health benefit premiums?

(a) Group health plan benefits must be continued on the same basis as coverage would have been provided if the employee had been continuously employed during the FMLA leave period. Therefore, any share of health plan premiums which had been paid by the employee prior to FMLA leave must continue to be paid by the employee during the FMLA leave period. If premiums are raised or lowered, the employee would be required to pay the new premium rates.

(b) If the FMLA leave is substituted paid leave, the employee's share of premiums must be paid by the method normally used during any paid leave, presumably as a payroll deduction.

(c) If FMLA leave is unpaid, the employer has a number of options for obtaining payment from the employee. The employer may require that payment be made to the employer or to the insurance carrier, but no additional charge may be added to the employee's premium payment for administrative expenses. The employer may require employees to pay their share of premium payments in any of the following ways:

(1) Payment would be due at the same time as it would be made if by payroll deduction;

(2) Payment would be due on the same schedule as payments are made under COBRA;

(3) Payment would be prepaid pursuant to a cafeteria plan at the employee's option;

(4) The employer's existing rules for payment by employees on "leave without pay" would be followed, providing that such rules do not require prepayment (*i.e.,* prior to the commencement of the leave) of the premiums that will become due during a period of unpaid FMLA leave; or,

(5) Another system voluntarily agreed to between the employer and the employee, which may include prepayment of premiums (*e.g.,* through increased payroll deductions when the need for the FMLA leave is foreseeable).

(d) The employer must provide the employee with advance written notice of the terms and conditions under which these payments must be made. (See § 825.301.)

(e) An employer may not require more of an employee using FMLA leave than the employer requires of other employees on "leave without pay."

§ 825.211 What special health benefits maintenance rules apply to multi-employer health plans?

(a) A multi-employer health plan is a plan to which more than one employer is required to contribute, and which is maintained pursuant to one or more collective barganing agreements between employee organization(s) and the employers.

(b) An employer under a multi-employer plan must continue to make contributions on behalf of an employee using FMLA leave as though the employee had been continuously employed, unless the plan contains an explicit FMLA provision for maintaining coverage such as through pooled contributions by all employers party to the plan.

(c) During the duration of an employee's FMLA leave, coverage by the health plan, and benefits provided pursuant to the plan, must continue at the level coverage would have been continued if the employee had continued to be employed.

(d) An employee using FMLA leave cannot be required to use "banked" hours or pay a greater premium than the employee would have been required to pay if the employee had been continuously employed.

§ 825.212 What are the consequences of an employee's failure to make timely health plan premium payments?

(a) While an employer may continue to maintain health benefits, an employer's obligations to maintain health insurance coverage ceases if an employee's premium payment is more than 30 days late. All other obligations of an employer under FMLA would continue; for example, the employer continues to have an obligation to reinstate an employee upon return from leave.

(b) The employer may recover the employee's share of any premium payments missed by the employee for any FMLA leave period during which the employer maintains health coverage by paying the employee's share after the premium payment is missed.

(c) If coverage lapses because an employee has not made required premium payments, upon the employee's return from FMLA leave the employer must still restore the employee to coverage/benefits equivalent to those the employee would have had if leave had not been taken and the premium payment(s) had not been missed. See § 825.215(d)(1)–(5). In such case, an employee may not be required to meet any qualification requirements imposed by the plan, including any new preexisting condition waiting period, to wait for an open season, or to pass a medical examination to obtain reinstatement of coverage.

§ 825.213 May an employer recover premiums it paid for maintaining "group health plan" coverage during FMLA leave?

(a) In addition to the circumstances discussed in § 825.212(b), an employer may recover its share of health plan premiums during a period of unpaid FMLA leave from an empoyee if the employee fails to return to work after the employee's FMLA leave entitlement has been exhausted or expires, *unless* the reason the employee does not return is due to:

(1) The continuation, recurrence, or onset of a serious health condition which would entitle the employee to leave under FMLA; or

(2) Other circumstances beyond the employee's control. Examples of other circumstances beyond the employee's control include such situations as where an employee's spouse is unexpectedly transferred to a job location more than 75 miles from the employee's worksite; a relative or individual other than an immediate family member has a serious health condition and the employee is needed to provide care; the employee is laid off while on leave; or, the employee is a "key employee" who decides not to return

to work upon being notified of the employer's intention to deny restoration because of substantial and grievous economic injury to the employer's operations and is not reinstated by the employer. Other circumstances beyond the employee's control would not include a situation where an employee desires to remain with a parent in a distant city even though the parent no longer requires the employee's care, or a mother's decision not to return to work to stay home with a newborn child.

(3) When an employee fails to return to work because of the continuation, recurrence, or onset of a serious health condition, thereby precluding the employer from recovering its (share of) health benefit premium payments made on the employee's behalf during a period of unpaid FMLA leave, the employer may require medical certification of the employee's or the family member's serious health condition. Such certification is not required unless requested by the employer. The employee is required to provide medical certification in a timely manner which, for purposes of this section, is within 30 days from the date of the employer's request. For purposes of medical certification, the employee may use the optional DOL form developed for this purpose (see § 825.306(a) and Appendix B of this part). If the employer requests medical certification and the employee does not provide such certification in a timely manner (within 30 days), the employer may recover the health benefit premiums it paid during the period of unpaid FMLA leave.

(4) When circumstances permit, the employer's right to recover its share of health premiums paid during periods of unpaid FMLA leave extends to the entire period of unpaid FMLA leave taken by the employee.

(b) An employee who returns to work for at least 30 calendar days is considered to have "returned" to work.

(c) When an employee elects or an employer requires paid leave to be substituted for FMLA leave, the employer may not recover its (share of) health insurance premiums for any period of FMLA leave covered by paid leave.

(d) The amount that self-insured employers may recover is limited to only the employer's share of allowable "Premiums" as would be calculated under COBRA, excluding the 2 percent fee for administrative costs.

(e) When an employee fails to return to work, except for the reasons stated in paragraphs (a)(1) and (a)(2) of this section, health premiums paid by the employer during a period of FMLA leave are a debt owed by the non-returning employee to the employer. The existence of this debt caused by the employee's failure to return to work does not alter the employer's responsibilities for coverage and, under a self-insurance plan, payment of claims incurred during the period of FMLA leave. In the circumstances where recovery is allowed, the employer may recover its share of health insurance premiums through deduction from any sums due to the employee (e.g., unpaid wages, vacation pay, profit sharing, *etc.*), provided such deductions do not otherwise violate applicable Federal or State wage payment or other laws. Alternatively, the employer may initiate legal action against the employee to recover its share of health insurance premiums.

(f) Under some circumstances an employer may elect to maintain other benefits, *e.g.,* life insurance, disability insurance, *etc.,* by paying the employee's (share of) premiums during periods of unpaid FMLA leave. For example, to ensure the employer can meet is responsibilities to provide equivalent benefits to the employee upon return from unpaid FMLA leave, it may be necessary that premiums be paid continuously to avoid a lapse of coverage. In such circumstances the employer is entitled to recover any premium payments made on the employee's behalf to maintain coverage of benefits during unpaid FMLA leave pursuant to the guidance set out in paragraphs (a) through (e) of this section, whether or not the employee returns from FMLA leave.

§ 825.214 What are an employee's rights on returning to work from FMLA leave?

(a) On return from FMLA leave, an employee is entitled to be returned to the same position the employee held when leave commenced, or to an equivalent position with equivalent benefits, pay, and other terms and conditions of employment.

(b) Ordinarily an employee will be restored to the same position the employee held prior to FMLA leave, with the same pay and benefits, if the position remains available. However, an employee has no right to return to the same position.

§ 825.215 What is an equivalent position?

(a) An equivalent position must have the same pay, benefits and working conditions, including privileges, perquisites and status. It must involve the same or substantially similar duties and responsibilities, which must entail substantially equivalent skill, effort, responsibility, and authority.

(b) If an employee is no longer qualified for the position because of the employee's inability to attend a necessary course, renew a license, fly a minimum number of hours, *etc.,* as a result of the leave, the employee shall be given a reasonable opportunity to fulfill those conditions upon return to work. If the employee is unable to perform the position because of a physical or mental condition, including the continuation of serious health condition, the employer's obligations may be governed by the Americans with Disabilities Act (ADA).

(c) Equivalent Pay. An employee is entitled to any unconditional pay increases which may have occurred during the FMLA leave period, such as cost of living increases. Pay increases conditioned upon seniority, length of service, or work performed would not have to be granted unless it is the employer's policy or practice to do so with respect to other employees on "leave without pay." In such case, any pay increase would be granted based on the employee's seniority, length of service, work performed, *etc.,* excluding the period of unpaid FMLA leave. An employee is entitled to be restored to a position with the same or equivalent pay premiums, such as a shift differential. If an employee departed from a position averaging ten hours of overtime (and corresponding overtime pay) each week, and employee is ordinarily entitled to such a position on return from FMLA leave.

(d) Equivalent Benefits. "Benefits" include all benefits provided or made available to employees by an employer, including group life insurance, health insurance, disability insurance, sick leave, annual leave, educational benefits, and pensions, regardless of whether such benefits are provided by a practice or written policy of an employer through an employee benefit plan as defined in Section 3(3) of the Employee Retirement Income Security Act of 1974, 29 U.S.C. 1002(3).

(1) At the end of an employee's FMLA leave, benefits must be resumed in the same manner and at the same levels as provided when the leave began, and subject to any changes in benefit levels that may have taken place during the period of FMLA leave affecting the entire workforce, unless otherwise elected by the employee. Upon return from FMLA leave, an employee cannot be required to requalify for any benefits the employee enjoyed before FMLA leave began. For example, if an employee was covered by a life insurance policy before taking leave but is not covered or coverage lapses during the period of unpaid FMLA leave, the employee cannot be required to meet any qualifications, such as taking a physical examination, in order to requalify for life insurance upon return from leave. Accordingly, some employers may find it necessary to modify life insurance and other benefits programs in order to restore employees to

equivalent benefits upon return from FMLA leave, make arrangements for continued payment of costs to maintain such benefits during unpaid FMLA leave, or pay these costs subject to recover form the employee on return from leave.

(2) An employee may, but is not entitled to, accrue any additional benefits or seniority during unpaid FMLA leave. Benefits accrued at the time leave began, however, (*e.g.,* paid vacation, sick or personal leave to the extent not substituted for FMLA leave) must be available to an employee upon return for leave.

(3) If an employee desires to continue life insurance, disability insurance, or other types of benefits for which he or she typically pays during unpaid FMLA leave, the employer is required to follow established policies or practices for continuing such benefits for other instances of leave without pay. If the employer has no established policy, the employee and the employer are encouraged to agree upon arrangements before FMLA leave begins.

(4) With respect to pension and other retirement plans, any period of FMLA leave will be treated as continued service (*i.e.,* no break in service) for purposes of vesting and eligibility to participate. If, for example, the plan requires an employee to be working on a specific date in order to be credited with a year of service for vesting or participation purposes, an employee on FMLA leave who subsequently returns to work shall be deemed to have been working on that date.

(5) Employees on unpaid FMLA leave are to be treated as if they continued to work for purposes of changes to benefit plans. They are entitled to changes in benefits plans, except those which may be dependent upon seniority or accrual during the leave period, immediately upon return from leave or to the same extent they would have qualified if no leave had been taken. (In this regard, § 825.209 addresses health benefits.)

(e) Equivalent Terms and Conditions of Employment. An equivalent position must have substantially similar duties, conditions, responsibilities, privileges and status as the employee's original position.

(1) The employee must be reinstated to the same or a geographically proximate worksite where the employee had previously been employed. If the employee's original worksite has been closed, the employee is entitled to the same rights as if the employee had not been on leave when the worksite closed. For example, if an employer transfers all employees from a closed worksite to a new worksite in a different city, the employee

on leave is also entitled to transfer under the same conditions as if he or she had continued to be employed.

(2) The employee is ordinarily entitled to return to the same shift or the same or an equivalent work schedule.

(3) The employee must have the same or an equivalent opportunity for bonuses, profit-sharing, and other similar discretionary and non-discretionary payments.

(4) FMLA does not prohibit an employer from accommodating an employee's request to be restored to a different shift, schedule, or position which better suits the employee's personal needs on return from leave, or to offer a promotion to a better position. However, an employee cannot be induced by the employer to accept a different position against the employee's wishes.

(f) The requirement that an employee be restored to the same or equivalent job with the same or equivalent pay, benefits, and terms and conditions of employment does not extend to intangible, unmeasurable aspects of the job. For example, the perceived loss of potential for future promotional opportunities is not encompassed in equivalent pay, benefits and working conditions; nor would any increased possibility of being subject to a future layoff. However, restoration to a job slated for layoff when the employee's original position is not would not meet the requirements of an equivalent position.

§ 825.216 Are there any limitations on an employer's obligation to reinstate an employee?

(a) An employee has no greater right to reinstatement or to other benefits and conditions of employment than if the employee had been continuously employed during the FMLA leave period. An employer must be able to show that an employee would not otherwise have been employed at the time reinstatement is requested in order to deny restoration to employment. For example, an employer would have the burden of proving that an employee would have been laid off during the FMLA leave period and, therefore, would not be entitled to reinstatement. If a shift has been eliminated, or overtime has been decreased, an employee would not be entitled to return to work that shift or the original overtime hours upon reinstatement. However, if a position on, for example, a night shift has been filled by another employee, the employee is entitled to return to the same shift on which employed before taking FMLA leave.

(b) If an employee was hired for a specific term or only to perform work on a discrete project, the employer has no obligation to restore the employee if the employment term or project is over and the employer would not otherwise have continued to employ the employee. On the other hand, if an employee was hired to perform work on a contract, and after that contract period the contract was awarded to another contractor, the successor contractor may be required to restore the employee if it is a successor employer. See § 825.107.

(c) In addition to the circumstances explained above, an employer may deny job restoration: to salaried eligible employees ("Key employees," as defined in paragraph (c) of § 825.218) if such denial is necessary to prevent substantial and grievous economic injury to the operations of the employer; or, to an employee who fails to provide a fitness for duty certificate to work under the conditions described in § 825.309.

§ 825.217 What is a "key employee"?

(a) A "key employee" is a salaried FMLA-eligible employee who is among the highest paid 10 percent of all the employees employed by the employer within 75 miles of the employee's worksite.

(b) The term "salaried" means "paid on a salary basis," as defined in 19 CFR 541.118. This is the Department of Labor regulation defining employees who may qualify as exempt from the minimum wage and overtime requirements of the FLSA as executive, administrative, and professional employees.

(c) A "key employee" must be "among the highest paid 10 percent" of all the employees—both salaried and non-salaried, eligible and ineligible—who are employed by the employer within 75 miles of the worksite.

(1) In determining which employees are among the highest paid 10 percent, year-to-date earnings are divided by weeks worked by the employee (including weeks in which paid leave was taken). Earnings include wages, premium pay, incentive pay, and non-discretionary and discretionary bonuses. Earnings do not include incentives whose value is determined at some future date, *e.g.,* stock options, or benefits or perquisites.

(2) The determination of whether a salaried employee is among the highest paid 10 percent shall be made at the time of the request for leave. No more than 10 percent of the employer's employees within 75 miles of the worksite may be "key employees."

§ 825.218 What does "substantial and grievous economic injury" mean?

(a) In order to deny restoration to a key employee, an employer must determine that the restoration of the employee to employment will cause "substantial and grievous economic injury" to the operations of the employer, not whether the absence of the employee will cause such substantial and grievous injury.

(b) An employer may take into account its ability to replace on a temporary basis (or temporarily do without) the employee on FMLA leave. If permanent replacement is unavoidable, the cost of then reinstating the employee can be considered in evaluating whether substantial and grievous economic injury will occur from restoration; in other words, the effect on the operations of the company of reinstating the employee in an equivalent position.

(c) A precise test cannot be set for the level of hardship or injury to the employer which must be sustained. If the reinstatement of a "key employee" threatens the economic viability of the firm that would constitute "substantial and grievous economic injury." A lesser injury which causes substantial, long-term economic injury would also be sufficient. Minor inconveniences and costs that the employer would experience in the normal course of doing business would certainly not constitute "substantial and grievous economic injury."

§ 825.219 What are the rights of a key employee?

(a) An employer who believes that reinstatement may be denied to a key employee, must give written notice to the employee at the time FMLA leave is requested (or when FMLA leave commences, if earlier) that he or she qualifies as a key employee. At the same time, the employer must also fully inform the employee of the potential consequences with respect to the reinstatement and maintenance of health benefits if the employer should determine the substantial and grievous economic injury to the employer's operations will result if the employee is reinstated from FMLA leave. If such notice cannot be given immediately because of the need to determine whether the employee is a key employee, it shall be given as soon as practicable after receipt of a request for leave (or the commencement of leave, if earlier). It is expected that in most circumstances there will be no desire that an employee be denied restoration after FMLA leave and, therefore, there would be no need to provide such notice. However, an employer who fails to provide such timely notice will lose its right to deny restoration even if substantial and grievous economic injury will result from reinstatement.

(b) As soon as an employer makes a good faith determination, based on the facts available, that substantial and grievous economic injury to its operations will result if a key employee who has requested or is using FMLA leave is reinstated, the employer shall notify the employee in writing of its determination, that it cannot deny FMLA leave, and that it intends to deny restoration to employment on completion of the FMLA leave. It is anticipated that an employer will ordinarily be able to give such notice prior to the employee starting leave. The employer must serve this notice either in person or by certified mail. This notice must explain the basis for the employer's finding that substantial and grievous economic injury will result, and must provide the employee a reasonable time in which to return to work, taking into account the circumstances, such as the length of the leave and the urgency of the need for the employee to return.

(c) If an employee does not return to work in response to the employer's notification of intent to deny restoration, the employee continues to be entitled to maintenance of health benefits and the employer may not recover its cost of health benefit premiums. A key employee's rights under FMLA continue unless and until the employee either gives notice that he or she no longer wishes to return to work, or the employer actually denies reinstatement at the conclusion of the leave period.

(d) After notice to an employee has been given that substantial and grievous economic injury will result if the employee is reinstated to employment, an employee is still entitled to request reinstatement at the end of the leave period even if the employee did not return to work in response to the employer's notice. The employer must then determine whether there will be substantial and grievous economic injury from reinstatement, based on the facts at that time. If it is determined that substantial and grievous economic injury will result, the employer shall notify the employee in writing (in person or by certified mail) of the denial of restoration.

§ 825.220 How are employees who exercise their rights protected?

(a) The FMLA prohibits interference with an employee's rights under the law, and with legal proceedings or inquiries relating to an employee's rights. More specifically, the law contains the following employee protections:

(1) An employer is prohibited from interfering with, restraining, or denying the exercise of (or attempts to exercise) any rights provided by the Act.

(2) An employer is prohibited from discharging or in any other way discriminating against any person (whether or not an employee) for opposing or complaining about any unlawful practice under the Act.

(3) All persons (whether or not employers) are prohibited from discharging or in any other way discriminating against any person (whether or not an employee) because that person has—

(i) Filed any charge, or has instituted (or caused to be instituted) any proceeding under or related to this Act;

(ii) Given, or is about to give, any information in connection with an inquiry or proceeding relating to a right under this Act;

(iii) Testified, or is about to testify, in any inquiry or proceeding relating to a right under this Act.

(b) Any violations of the Act or of these regulations constitute interfering with, restraining, or denying the exercise of rights provided by the Act. "Interfering with" the exercise of an employee's rights would include, for example, not only refusing to authorize FMLA leave, but discouraging an employee from using such leave. It would also include manipulation by an employer to avoid responsibilities under FMLA, such as unnecessarily transferring employees from one worksite to another in order to keep worksites below the 50-employee threshold for employee eligibility under the Act.

(c) An employer is prohibited from discriminating against employees who use FMLA leave. For example, if an employee substitutes paid leave for unpaid FMLA leave and the employer does not normally require written notice or certification for use of paid leave, an employer cannot require written notice or certification for the *paid* FMLA leave. Similarly, if an employee on leave without pay would otherwise be entitled to full benefits (other than health benefits), the same benefits would be required to be provided to an employee on unpaid FMLA leave. By the same token, employers cannot use the taking of FMLA leave as a negative factor in employment actions, such as promotions or disciplinary actions; nor can FMLA leave be counted under "no fault" attendance policies.

(d) Employees cannot waive their rights under FMLA. For example, employees (or their collective bargaining representatives) cannot "trade off" the right to take FMLA leave against some other benefit offered by the employer. Employers are prohibited from inducing an employee to waive rights under the Act.

(e) Individuals, and not merely employees, are protected from retaliation for opposing (*e.g.*, file a complaint about) any practice which is unlawful under the Act. They are similarly protected if they oppose any practice which they reasonably believe to be a violation of the Act or regulations.

Subpart C—How do Employees Learn of Their FMLA Rights and Obligations, and What Can an Employer Require of an Employee?

§ 825.300 What posting requirements does the Act place on employers?

(a) Every employer subject to the FMLA is required to post and keep posted on its premises, in conspicuous places where employees are employed, a notice explaining the Act's provisions and providing information concerning the procedures for filing complaints of violations of the Act with the Wage and Hour Division. The notice must be posted prominently where it can be readily seen by employees and applicants for employment. Employers may duplicate the text of the notice contained in Appendix C of this part, or copies of the required notice may be obtained from local offices of the Wage and Hour Division. When duplicating the text of the notice, no reproduction of the notice smaller than 8 1/2 inches by 11 inches will satisfy the posting requirements of this regulation, and the reproduction must contain fully legible text.

(b) An employer that willfully violates the posting requirement may be assessed a civil money penalty by the Wage and Hour Division not to exceed $100 for each separate offense. Furthermore, an employer that fails to post the required notice cannot take any adverse action against an employee, including denying FMLA leave, for failing to furnish the employer with advance notice of a need to take FMLA leave.

(c) Where an employer's workforce is comprised of a significant portion of workers who are not literate in English, the employer shall be responsible for providing the information required by the notice provisions of this regulation in a language in which the employees are literate.

§ 825.301 What other notices to employees are required of employers under the FMLA?

(a) If an employer has any written guidance to employees concerning employee benefits or leave rights, such as in an employee handbook, information concerning FMLA entitlements and employee obligations under the FMLA must be included in the handbook or other document. For example, if an employer provides an employee handbook to all employees that describes the employer's policies regarding leave, wages, attendance, and similar matters, the handbook must incorporate information on FMLA rights and responsibilities and the employer's policies regarding the FMLA. Information publications describing the Act's provisions are available from local offices of the Wage and Hour Division and may be incorporated in such employer handbooks or written policies.

(b) If an employer does not have written policies, manuals, or handbooks describing employee benefits and leave provisions, the employer shall provide written guidance to an employee concerning all the employee's rights and obligations under the FMLA whenever an employee requests leave under the FMLA. Employers may duplicate and provide the employee a copy of the FMLA Fact Sheet available from the nearest office of the Wage and Hour Division to provide such guidance.

(c) In addition, when an employee provides notice of the need for FMLA leave, the employer shall provide the employee with notice detailing the specific expectations and obligations of the employee and explaining any consequences of a failure to meet these obligations. Such specific notice should include, as appropriate:

(1) that the leave will be counted against their annual FMLA leave entitlement;

(2) any requirements for the employee to furnish medical certification of a serious health condition and the consequences of failing to do so (see § 825.305);

(3) the employee's right to substitute paid leave and whether the employer will require the substitution of paid leave, and the conditions related to any substitution;

(4) any requirement for the employee to make any premium payments to maintain health benefits and the arrangements for making such payments (sse § 825.210);

(5) any requirement for the employee to present a fitness-for-duty certificate to be restored to employment (see § 825.309);

(6) their status as a "key employee" and the potential consequence that restoration may be denied following FMLA leave, explaining the conditions required for such denial (see § 825.218);

(7) the employee's right to restoration to the same or an equivalent job upon return from leave (see §§ 825.214 and 825.604); and,

(8) the employee's potential liability for payment of health insurance premiums paid by the employer during the employee's unpaid FMLA leave if the employee fails to return to work after taking FMLA leave (see § 825.213). This specific notice may include other information—*e.g.,* whether the employer will require periodic reports of the employee's status and intent to return to work, or will require any recertification relating to a serious health condition—but is not required to do so. A prototype notice is available from local offices of the Department of Labor's Wage and Hour Division, which employers may adapt for their optional use to meet these specific notice requirements.

(d) Employers are also expected to responsively answer questions from employees concerning their rights and responsibilities under the FMLA.

§ 825.302 What notice does an employee have to give an employer when the need for FMLA leave is foreseeable?

(a) An employee must provide the employer at last 30 days advance notice before FMLA leave is to begin if the need for the leave is foreseeable based on an expected birth, placement for adoption or foster care, or planned medical treatment for a serious health condition of the employee or of a family member. If 30 days notice is not practicable, such as because of a lack of knowledge of approximately when leave will be required to begin, a change in circumstances, or a medical emergency, notice must be given as soon as practicable. For example, an employee's health condition may require leave to commence earlier than anticipated before the birth of a child. similarly, little opportunity for notice may be given before placement for adoption.

(b) "As soon as practicable" means as soon as both possible and practical, taking into account all of the acts and circumstances in the individual case. For foreseeable leave where it is not possible to give as much as 30 days notice, "as soon as practicable" ordinarily would mean at least verbal notification to the employer within one or two business days of when the need for leave becomes known to the employee.

(c) An employee shall provide at least verbal notice sufficient to make the employer aware that the employee needs FMLA qualifying leave, and the anticipated timing and duration of the leave. The employee need not expressly assert rights under the FMLA or even mention the FMLA, but may only state that leave is needed for an expected birth or adoption, for example. The employer should inquire further of the employee if it is necessary to have more information about whether FMLA leave is being sought by the employee, and obtain the necessary details of the leave to be taken. In the case of medical conditions, the employer may find it necessary to inquire further to determine if the leave is because of a serious health condition and may request medical certification to support the need for such leave (see § 825.305).

(d) An employer may also require an employee to comply with the employer's usual and customary notice and procedural requirements for requesting leave without pay. For example, an employer may require that written notice set forth the reasons for the requested leave, the anticipated duration of the leave, and the anticipated start of the leave. However, failure to follow such internal employer procedures will not permit an employer to disallow an employee's taking FMLA leave if the employee gives timely verbal or other notice.

(e) When planning medical treatment, the employee should consult with the employer and make a reasonable effort to schedule the leave so as not to disrupt unduly the employer's operations, subject to the approval of the health care provider. Employees are ordinarily expected to consult with their employers prior to the scheduling of treatment in order to work out a treatment schedule which best suits the needs of both the employer and the employee. In any event, when notice is given of the need for leave, an employer may, for justifiable cause, require an employee to attempt to reschedule treatment, subject to the ability of the health care provider to reschedule the treatment and the approval of the health care provider as to any modification of the treatment schedule.

(f) In the case of a request for intermittent leave or leave on a reduced leave schedule which is medically necessary, an employee shall advise the employer, upon request, of the reasons why the intermittent/reduced leave schedule is necessary and of the schedule for treatment, if applicable. The employee and employer shall attempt to work out a schedule which meets the employee's needs without unduly disrupting the employer's operations, subject to the approval of the health care provider.

(g) An employer may waive employees' FMLA notice requirements. In addition, an employer may not require compliance with stricter FMLA notice requirements where the provision of a collective bargaining agreement, State law, or applicable leave plan allow less advance notice to the employer.

§ 825.303 What are the requirements for an employee to furnish notice to an employer where the need for FMLA leave is not foreseeable?

(a) When the need for leave, or its approximate timing, is not foreseeable, an employee should give notice to the employer of the need for FMLA leave as soon as practicable under the facts and circumstances of the particular case. It is expected that an employee will give notice to the employer within no more than one or two working days of learning of the need for leave, except in extraordinary circumstances. In the case of a medical emergency requiring leave because of an employee's own serious health condition or to care for a family member with a serious health condition, written advance notice pursuant to an employer's internal rules and procedures cannot be required when FMLA leave is involved.

(b) The employee should provid notice to the employer either in person or by telephone, telegraph, facsimile ("fax") machine or other electronic means. Notice may be given by the employee's representative (*e.g.*, a spouse, family member or other responsible party) if the employee is unable to do so personally. The employer will be expected to obtain any additional required information through informal means. The employee or representative will be expected to provide more information when it can readily be accomplished as a practical matter, taking into consideration the exigencies of the situation.

§ 825.304 What recourse do employers have if employees fail to provide the required notice?

(a) An employer may waive employees' FMLA notice obligations or the employer's own internal rules on leave notice requirements.

(b) If an employee fails to give 30 days notice for foreseeable leave with no reasonable excuse for the delay, the employer may deny the taking of FMLA leave until at least 30 days after the date the employee provides notice to the employer of the need for FMLA leave.

(c) In all cases, in order for the onset of an employee's FMLA leave to be delayed due to lack of required notice, it must be clear that the employee had actual notice of the FMLA notice requirements. This condition would be satisfied by the employer's proper posting of the required notice at the worksite where the employee is employed. Furthermore, the need for leave and the approximate date leave would be taken must have been clearly foreseeable to the employee 30 days in advance of the leave. For example, knowledge that an employee would receive a telephone call about the availability of a child for adoption at some unknown point in the future would not be sufficient.

(d) Where the employee elects or the employer requires use of paid leave, or where the employer has a less stringent policy regarding requests for "leave without pay," such as for leave of short duration, the employer's usual policy for notification for such leave shall apply.

(e) If an employer does not waive employees' notice requirements and chooses to take action against an employee for violating these notice requirements, the employer's policies and procedures must be uniformly applied in similar circumstances.

§ 825.305 When must an employee provide medical certification to support a FMLA leave request?

(a) An employer may require that an employee's request for leave to care for the employee's seriously-ill spouse, son, daughter, or parent, or due to the employee's own serious health condition that makes the employee unable to perform the functions of the employee's position, be supported by a certification issued by the health care provider of the employee or the employee's ill family member. An employer must give written notice of a requirement for medical certification (see § 825.301) in a particular case, but an employer's verbal request to an employee to furnish any subsequent medical certification is sufficient. The employee must provide the requested certification to the employer within the time frame requested by the employer (which must allow at least 15 calendar days after the employer's request), unless it is not practicable under the particular circumstances to do so despite the employee's diligent, good faith efforts.

(b) In most cases, the employer should request that an employee furnish certification from a health care provider at the time the employee requests leave or soon after the leave is requested, or, in the case of unforeseen leave, soon after the leave commences. The employer may request certification at some later date if the employer later has reason to question the appropriateness of the leave or its duration.

(c) At the time the employer requests certification, the employer must also advise an employee of the anticipated consequences of an employee's failure to provide adequate certification. The employer shall advise an employee whenever the employer finds a certification incomplete, and provide the employee a reasonable opportunity to cure any such deficiency.

§ 825.306 How much information may be required in medical certifications of a serious health condition?

(a) DOL has developed an optional form for employee's use in obtaining medical certification from health care providers that meets FMLA's certification requirements. (See Appendix B to these regulations.) This option form reflects certification requirements so as to permit the health care provider to furnish appropriate medical information within his or her knowledge. This form, or another form containing the same basic information, may be used by the employer; however, no additional information may be required. The form identifies the practitioner and type of medical practice (including pertinent specialization, if any), makes maximum use of checklist entries for ease in completing the form, and contains required entries for:

(1) The date the serious health condition commenced and the health care provider's best medical judgment concerning the probable duration of the condition;

(2) Diagnosis of the serious health condition;

(3) A brief statement of the regimen of treatment prescribed for the condition by the health care provider (including estimated number of visits, nature, frequency and duration of treatment, including treatment by another provider of health services on referral by or order of the health care provider); and

(4) Indication of whether inpatient hospitalization is required.

(b) For medical leave because of the employee's own serious health condition, the health care provider's certification must also include either a statement that the employee is unable to perform work of any kind, or a statement that the employee is unable to perform the essential functions of the employee's position, based on either information provided via a statement from the employer if the essential functions of the employee's position, or, if not provided, discussion with the employee about the employee's job functions. (See § 825.115.)

(c) For family leave to care for a seriously-ill family member, the health care provider's certification must also include a statement that the patient requires assistance for basic medical, hygiene, nutritional needs, safety or transportation, or that the employee's presence would be beneficial or desirable for the care of the family member, which may include psychological comfort. The employee is required to indicate on the form the care he/she will provide and an estimate of the time period. (See § 825.116.)

(d) The treatment regimen and other information in the certification should satisfy the requirement that—if leave must be taken intermittently or on a reduced leave schedule because of the employee's own serious health condition or a seriously-ill family member—the certification include:

(1) A statement of the medical necessity for such leave (see § 825.117); or,

(2) That the leave is necessary to care for the child, parent, or spouse who has a serious health condition, or will assist in the family member's recovery, and

(3) The expected duration and schedule of the intermittent or reduced leave schedule. (See § 825.116.)

§ 825.307 What can an employer do if it questions the adequacy of a medical certification?

(a) If an employee submits a complete certification signed by the health care provider, the employer may not request additional information from the employee's health care provider. Rather, an employer who has reason to doubt the validity of a medical certification may require the employee to obtain a second opinion at the employer's expense. The employer is permitted to designate the health care provider to furnish the second opinion, but the selected health care provider cannot be employed on a regular basis by the employer.

(b) The employer may not regularly contract with or otherwise regularly utilize the services of the health care provider furnishing the second opinion unless the employer is located in an area where access to health care is extremely limited (*e.g.*, a rural area where no more than one or two doctors practice in the relevant specialty in the vicinity).

(c) If the opinions of the employee's and the employer's designated health care providers differ, the employer may require the employee to obtain certification from a third health care provider, again at the employer's expense. This third opinion shall be final and binding. The third health care provider must be designated or approved jointly by the employer and the employee. The employer and the employee must each act in good faith to attempt to reach agreement on whom to select for the third opinion provider. If the employer does not attempt in good faith to reach agreement, the employer will be bound by the first certification. If the employee does not attempt in good faith to reach agreement, the employee will be bound by the second certification. For example, an employee who refuses to agree to see a doctor in the specialty in question may be failing to act in good faith. On the other hand, an employer that refuses to agree to any doctor on a list of specialists in the appropriate field provided by the employee and whom the employee has not previously consulted may be failing to act in good faith.

§ 825.308 Under what circumstances can an employer request subsequent recertifications of medical conditions to support leave requests?

An employer may request recertification at any reasonable interval, but not more often than every 30 days, unless:

(a) The employee requests an extension of leave;

(b) Circumstances described by the original certification have changed significantly (*e.g.*, the duration of the illness, the nature of the illness, complications); or

(c) The employer receives information that casts doubt upon the continuing validity of the certification.

(d) When an employee is unable to return to work after FMLA leave because of the continuation, recurrence, or onset of a serious health condition, thereby preventing the employer from recovering its share of health benefit premium payments made on the employee's behalf during a period of unpaid FMLA leave, the employer may require medical certification of the employee's or the family member's serious health condition. (See § 825.213(a)(3).)

§ 825.309 What notice may an employer require regarding an employee's intent to return to work?

(a) An employer may require an employee on FMLA leave to report periodically on the employee's status and intent to return to work. The employer's policy regarding such reports may not be discriminatory and must take into account all of the relevant facts and circumstances related to the individual employee's leave situation.

(b) If an employee gives unequivocal notice of intent not to return to work, the employer's obligations under FMLA to maintain health benefits (subject to COBRA requirements) and to restore the employee cease. However, these obligations continue if an employee indicates he or she may be unable to return to work but expresses a continuing desire to do so.

§ 825.310 Under what circumstances may an employer require that an employee submit a medical certification that the employee is able (or unable) to return to work (*e.g.*, a "fitness-for-duty" report)?

(a) As a condition of restoring an employee whose FMLA leave was occasioned by the employee's own serious health condition that made the employee unable to perform the employee's job, an employer may have uniformly-applied policy or practice that requires all employees who take leave for such conditions to obtain and present certification from the health care provider that the employee is able to resume work. This does not mean that the employer's policy or practice must require fitness-for-duty certification from all employees who are absent due to a serious health condition, but an employer requiring any fitness for duty certifications must have a uniformly-applied policy that is based on, for example, the nature of the illness or the duration of the absence.

(b) An employer may seek fitness-for-duty certification only with regard to the particular health condition that caused the employee's need for FMLA leave. The certification itself need only be a simple statement of an employee's ability to return to work. If State or local law or the terms of a collective bargaining agreement govern an employee's return to work, those provisions shall be applied. Similarly, requirements under the Americans with Disabilities Act (ADA) that any return-to-work physical be job-related must be complied with.

(c) The notice that employers are required to give to each employee requesting FMLA leave regarding their FMLA rights and obligations (see § 825.301) shall advise the employee if the employer will require fitness-for-duty certification to return to work. If the employer has a handbook explaining employment policies and benefits, the handbook should explain the employer's general policy regarding any requirement for fitness-for-duty certification to return to work. Specific notice shall also be given to any employee from whom fitness-for-duty certification will be required either at the time leave is requested or immediately after leave commences and the employer is advised of the medical circumstances requiring the leave, unless the employee's condition changes from one that did not previously require certification pursuant to the employer's practice or policy. No second or third fitness-for-duty certification may be required.

(d) An employer may deny restoration to employment until an employee submits a required fitness-for-duty certification unless the employer has failed to provide the notices required in paragraph (c) of this section.

§ 825.311 What happens if an employee fails to satisfy the medical certification requirements?

(a) In the case of foreseeable leave, an employee who fails to provide timely certification after being requested by the employer to furnish such certification (*e.g.,* within 15 calendar days, if practicable), may be denied the taking of leave until the required certification is provided.

(b) When the need for leave is *not* foreseeable, an employee must provide certification within the time frame requested by the employer (which must allow at least 15 days after the employer's request) *or* as soon as reasonably possible under the particular facts and circumstances. In the case of a medical emergency, it may not be practicable for an employee to provide the required certification within 15 calendar days. If an employee fails to provide a medical certification within a reasonable time under the pertinent circumstances, the employer may deny the employee's continuation of leave.

(c) When requested by the employer pursuant to a uniformly applied policy, the employee must provide medical certification at the time the employee seeks reinstatement at the end of FMLA leave taken for the employee's serious health condition, that the employee is fit for duty and able to return to work. The employer may deny restoration until the certification is provided. (See § 825.309.)

§ 825.312 Under what circumstances can a covered employer refuse to provide FMLA leave or reinstatement to eligible employees?

(a) If an employee fails to give timely advance notice when the need for FMLA leave is foreseeable, the employer may deny the taking of FMLA leave until 30 days after the date the employee provides notice to the employer of the need for FMLA leave. (See § 825.302.)

(b) If an employee fails to provide in a timely manner a requested medical certification to substantiate the need for FMLA leave due to a serious health condition, an employer may deny FMLA leave until an employee submits the certificate. (See §§ 825.305 and 825.310.)

(c) If an employee fails to provide a requested fitness-for-duty certification to return to work, an employer may deny restoration until the employee submits the certificate. (See §§ 825.309 and 825.310.)

(d) An employee has no greater right to reinstatement or to other benefits and conditions of employment than if the employee had been continuously employed during the FMLA leave period. An employer must be able to show, when an employee requests reinstatement, that the employee would not otherwise have been employed if leave had not been taken in order to deny restoration to employment. (See § 825.216.)

(e) If an employee unequivocally advises the employer that the employee does not intend to return to work, the employment relationship is deemed terminated, and the employee's entitled to reinstatement, continued leave, and health benefits ceases. An employer may require an employee on FMLA leave to report periodically on the employee's status and intention to return to work. (See § 825.309.)

(f) An employer may deny restoration to employment, but not the taking of FMLA leavc and the maintenance of health benefits, to an eligible employee only under the terms of the "key employee" exemption. Denial of reinstatement must be necessary to prevent "substantial and grievous economic injury" to the employer's operations. The employer must notify the employee of the employee's status as a "key employee" and of the employer's intent to deny reinstatement on that basis when the employer makes these determinations. If leave has started, the employee must be given a reasonable opportunity to return to work after being so notified. (See § 825.220.)

(g) An employee who fraudulently obtains FMLA leave from an employer is not protected by FMLA's job restoration or maintenance of health benefits provisions.

(h) If the employer has a uniformly-applied policy governing outside or supplemental employment, such a policy may continue to apply to an employee while on FMLA leave. An employer which does not have such a policy may not deny benefits to which an employee is entitled under FMLA on this basis unless the FMLA leave was fraudulently obtained as in paragraph (g) of this section.

Subpart D— What Enforcement Mechanisms does FMLA Provide?

§ 825.400 What can employees do who believe that their rights under FMLA have been violated?

(a) The employee has the choice of:

(1) filing, or having another person file on his or her behalf, a complaint with the Secretary of Labor, or

(2) Filing a private lawsuit pursuant to section 107 of FMLA.

(b) If the employee files a private lawsuit, it must be filed within two years after the last action which the employee contends was in violation of the Act, or three years if the violation was willful.

(c) If an employer has violated one or more provisions of FMLA, and if justified by the facts of a particular case, an employee may receive one or more of the following: wages, employment benefits, or other compensation denied or lost to such employee by reason of the violation; or, where no such tangible loss has occurred, such as when FMLA leave was unlawfully denied, any actual monetary loss sustained by the employee as direct result of the violation, such as the cost of providing care, up to a sum equal to 12 weeks of wages for the employee. In addition, the employee may be entitled to interest on such sum, calculated at the prevailing rate. An amount equalling the preceding sums my also be awarded as liquidated damages unless such amount is reduced by the court because the violation was in good faith and the employer had reasonable grounds for believing the employer had not violated the Act. When appropriate, the employee may also receive employment, reinstatement and promotion, and reimbursement for the cost of the action. Reasonable attorney's and expert witness fees are paid by an employer found in violation.

§ 825.401 Where can an employee file a complaint of FMLA violations with the Federal government?

(a) A complaint may be filed in person, by mail or by telephone, with the Wage and Hour Division, Employment Standards Administration, U.S. Department of Labor. A complaint may be filed at any local office of the Wage and Hour Division; the address and telephone number of local offices may be found in telephone directories.

(b) A complaint filed with the Secretary of Labor should be filed within a reasonable time of when the employee discovers that his or her FMLA rights have been violated. In no event may a complaint be filed more than two years after the action which is alleged to be a violation of FMLA occurred, or three years in the case of a willful violation.

(c) No particular form of complaint is required, except that a complaint must be reduced to writing and should include a full statement of the acts and/or omissions, with pertinent dates, which are believed to constitute the violation.

§ 825.402 How is an employer notified of a violation of the posting requirement?

Section 825.300 describes the requirements for covered employers to post a notice for employees that explains the Act's provisions. If a representative of the Department of Labor determines that an employer has committed a willful violation of this posting requirement, and that the imposition of a civil money penalty for such violation is appropriate, the representative may issue and serve a notice of penalty on such employer in person or by certified mail. Where service by certified mail is not accepted, notice shall be deemed received on the date of attempted delivery. Where service is not accepted, the notice may bc served by regular mail.

§ 825.403 How may an employer appeal the assessment of a penalty for willful violation of the posting requirement?

(a) An employer may obtain a review of the assessment of penalty from the Wage and Hour Regional Administrator for the region in which the alleged violation(s) occurred. If the employer does not seek such a review or fails to do so in a timely manner, the notice of thc penalty constitutes the final ruling of the Secretary of Labor.

(b) To obtain review, an employer may file a petition with the Wage and Hour Regional Administrator for the region in which the alleged violations occurred. No particular form of petition for review is required, except that the petition must be in writing, should contain the legal and factual bases for the petition, and must be mailed to the Regional Administrator within 15 days of receipt of the notice of penalty. The employer may request an oral hearing which may be conducted by telephone.

(c) The decision of the Regional Administrator constitutes the final order of the Secretary.

§ 825.404 What are the consequences of an employer not paying the penalty assessment after a final order is issued?

The Regional Administrator may seek to recover the unpaid penalty pursuant to the Debt Collection Act (DCA), 31 U.S.C. 3711 *et seq.*, and, in addition to seeking recovery of the unpaid final order, may seek interest and penalties as provided under the DCA. The final order may also be referred to the Solicitor of Labor for collection. The Secretary may file suit in any court of competent jurisdiction to recover the monies due as a result of the unpaid final order, interest, and penalties.

Subpart E—What Records Must Be Kept to Comply with the FMLA?

§ 825.500 What records must an employer keep to comply with the FMLA?

(a) FMLA provides that employers shall make, keep, and preserve records pertaining to their obligations under the Act in accordance with the recordkeeping requirements of section 11(c) of the Fair Labor Standards Act (FLSA) and in accordance with these regulations. FMLA also restricts the authority of the Department of Labor to require any employer or plan, fund or program to submit books or records more than once during any 12-month period unless the Department has reasonable cause to believe a violation of the FMLA exists or the DOL is investigating a complaint. These regulations establish no requirement for the submission of any records unless specifically requested by a Departmental official.

(b) *Form of records.* No particular order or form of records is required. These regulations establish *no* requirement that any employer revise its computerized payroll or personnel records systems to comply. However, employers must keep the records specified by these regulations for no less than three years and make them available for inspection, copying, and transcription by representatives of the Department of Labor upon request. The records may be maintained and preserved on microfilm or other basic source document of an automated date processing memory provided that adequate projection or viewing equipment is available, that the reproductions are clear and identifiable by date or pay period,m and that extensions or transcriptions of the information required herein can be and are made available upon request. Records kept in computer form must be made available for transcription or copying.

(c) *Items required.* Records kept in accordance with this part must disclose the following:

(1) Basic payroll and identifying employee data, including name, address, and occupation; rate or basis of pay and terms of compensation; daily and weekly hours worked per pay period; additions to or deductions from wages; and total compensation paid.

(2) Dates FMLA leave is taken by employees (*e.g.*, available from time records, requests for leave, etc., if so designated). Leave must be designated in records as FMLA leave; leave so designated may *not* include leave provided under State law or an employer plan which is not covered by FMLA.

(3) If FMLA leave is taken in increments of less than one full day, the hours of the leave.

(4) Copies of employee notices of leave furnished to the employer under FMLA, if in writing, and copies of all general and specific notices given to employees as required under FMLA and these regulations (*e.g.*, copies may be maintained in employee personnel files).

(5) Any documents (including written and electronic records) describing employee benefits or employer policies and practices regarding the taking of paid and unpaid leaves.

(6) Premium payments of employee benefits.

(7) Records of any dispute between the employer and an employee regarding designation of leave as FMLA leave, including any written statement from the employer or employee of the reasons for the designation and for the disagreement.

(d) If employees are not subject to FLSA's recordkeeping regulations for purposes of minimum wage or overtime compliance (*i.,e.*, not covered by or exempt from FLSA), an employer need not keep a record of actual hours worked (as otherwise required under FLSA, 29 CFR 516.2(a)(7), provided that:

(1) eligibility for FMLA leave is presumed for any employee who has been employed for at least 12 months; and

(2) with respect to employees who take FMLA leave intermittently or on a reduced leave schedule, the employer and employee agree on the employee's normal schedule or average hours worked each week and reduce their agreement to a written record maintained in accordance with paragraph (b) of this section.

(e) Records and documents relating to medical certifications, recertifications or medical histories of employees or employees' family members, shall be maintained in separate files/records and be treated as confidential medical records, except that:

(1) Supervisors and managers may be informed regarding necessary restrictions on the work or duties of an employee and necessary accommodations;

(2) First aid and safety personnel may be informed (when appropriate) if the employee's physical or medical condition might require emergency treatment; and

(3) Government officials investigating compliance with FMLA (or other pertinent law) shall be provided relevant information upon request.

Subpart F—What Special Rules Apply to Employees of Schools?

§ 825.600 To whom do the special rules apply?

(a) Certain special rules apply to employees of "local educational agencies," including public school boards and elementary and secondary schools under their jurisdiction, and private elementary and secondary schools. The special rules do not apply to other kinds of educational institutions, such as colleges and universities, trade schools, and pre-schools.

(b) Educational institutions are covered by FMLA (and these special rules) and the Act's 50-employee coverage test does not apply. The usual requirements for employees to be "eligible" do apply, however, including employment at a worksite where at least 50 employees are employed within 75 miles. For example, employees of a rural school would not be eligible for FMLA leave if the school has fewer than 50 employees and there are no other schools under the jurisdiction of the same employer (usually, a school board) within 75 miles.

(c) The special rules affect the taking of intermittent leave or leave on a reduced leave schedule, or leave near the end of an academic term (semester), by instructional employees. "Instructional employees" are those whose principal function is to teach and instruct students in a class, a small group, or any individual setting. This term includes not only teachers, but also athletic coaches, driving instructors, and special education assistants such as signers for the hearing impaired. It does not include, and the special rules do not apply to, teacher assistants or aides who do not have as their principal job actual teaching or instructing, nor does it include auxiliary personnel such as counselors, psychologists, or curriculum specialists. It also does not include cafeteria workers, maintenance workers, or bus drivers.

(d) Special rules which apply to restoration to an equivalent position apply to all employees of local educational agencies.

§ 825.601 What limitations apply to the taking of intermittent leave or leave on a reduced leave schedule?

(a)(1) If an eligible instructional employee requests intermittent leave or leave on a reduced leave schedule to care for a family member, or for the employee's own serious health condition, which is foreseeable based on planned medical treatment, and the employee would be on leave for more than 20 percent of the total number of working days over the period the leave would extend, the employer may require the employee to choose either to:

(i) Take leave for a period or periods of a particular duration, not greater than the duration of the planned treatment; or

(ii) Transfer temporarily to an available alternative position for which the employee is qualified, which has equivalent pay and benefits and which better accommodates recurring periods of leave than does the employee's regular position.

(2) These rules apply only to a leave involving more than 20 percent of the working days during the period over which the leave extends. For example, if an instructional employee who normally works five days each week needs to take two days of FMLA leave per week over a period of several weeks, the special rules would apply. Employees taking leave which constitutes 20 percent or less of the working days during the leave period would be subject to the usual rules for taking intermittent or reduced schedule leave in §§ 825.117 and 825.203. The usual rules would apply, for example, to such an employee who needs only one day of leave per week. "Periods of a particular duration" means a block, or blocks, of time beginning no earlier than the first day for which leave is needed and ending no later than the last day on which leave is needed, and may include one uninterrupted period of leave.

(b) If an instructional employee does not give required notice of foreseeable FMLA leave (see § 825.302) to be taken intermittently or on a reduced leave schedule, the employer may require the employee to take leave of a particular duration, or to transfer temporarily to an alternative position. Alternatively, the employer may require the employee to delay the taking of leave until the notice provision is met. However, an employer may not have stricter FMLA notice requirements than are required for other employees taking paid or unpaid leave, as appropriate.

§ 825.602 What limitations apply to the taking of leave near the end of an academic term?

(a) There are also different rules for instructional employees who begin leave more than five weeks before the end of a term, less than five weeks before the end of a term, and less than three weeks before the end of a term. Regular rules apply except in circumstances when:

(1) An instructional employee begins leave more than five weeks before the end of a term. The employer may require the employee to continue taking leave until the end of the term if–

(i) The leave will last at least three weeks, and

(ii) The employee would return to work during the two-week period before the end of the term.

(2) Thc cmployce bcgins lcavc for a purpose other than the employee's own serious health condition *during* the five-week period before the end of a term. The employer may require the employee to continue taking leave until the end of the term if–

(i) The leave will last more than two weeks, and

(ii) The employee would return to work during the two-week period before the end of the term.

(3) The employee begins leave for a purpose other than the employee's own serious health condition during the three-week period before the end of a term, and the leave will last more than five working days. The employer may require the employee to continue taking leave until the end of the term.

(b) For purposes of these provisions, "academic term" means the school semester, which typically ends near the end of the calendar year and the end of spring each school year. In no case may a school have more than two academic terms or semesters each year for purposes of FMLA. An example of leave falling within these provisions would be where an employee plans two weeks of leave to care for a family member which will begin three weeks before the end of the term. In that situation, the employer could require the employee to say out on leave until the end of the term.

§ 825.603 Is all leave taken during "periods of a particular duration" counted against the FMLA leave entitlement?

(a) If an employee chooses, or is required, to take leave for "periods of a particular duration" in the case of intermittent or reduced schedule leave, or is required to continue taking leave until the end of school term in the case of leave taken near the end of the term, the entire period of leave taken will count as FMLA leave.

(b) In the case of an employee who is required to take leave until the end of an academic term, if the employee's leave entitlement under FMLA ends before the involuntary leave period is completed, the employer is required to maintain health benefits and must restore the employee and provide other FMLA entitlements when the period of leave ends.

§ 825.604 What special rules apply to restoration to "an equivalent position?"

The determination of how an employee is to be restored to "an equivalent position" upon return from FMLA leave will be made on the basis of "established school board policies and practices, private school policies and practices, and collective bargaining agreements." The "established policies" and collective bargaining agreements used as a basis for restoration must be in writing, must be made known to the employee prior to the taking of FMLA leave, and must clearly explain thc cmployce's restoration rights upon return from leave. Any established policy which is used as the basis for restoration of an employee to "an equivalent position" must provide substantially the same protections as provided in the Act for reinstated employees. In other words, the policy or collective bargaining agreement must provide for restoration to an "equivalent position" with equivalent employment benefits, pay, and other terms and conditions of employment.

Subpart G—How Do Other Laws, Employer Practices, and Collective Bargaining Agreements Affect Employee Rights Under FMLA?

§ 825.700 What if an employer provides more generous benefits than required by FMLA?

(a) An employer must observe any employment benefit program or plan that provides greater family or medical leave rights to employees than the rights established by the FMLA. Conversely, the rights established by the Act may not be diminished by any employment benefit program or plan. For example, provisions of a CBA which, because of seniority or otherwise, provide for reinstatement to a position that is not equivalent (e.g., provides lesser pay) are superseded by FMLA. If an employer provides greater unpaid family leave rights than are afforded by FMLA, the employer is not required to extend additional rights afforded by FMLA, such as maintenance of health benefits (other than through COBRA), to the additional leave period not covered by FMLA. If an employee takes paid leave and neither the employee nor the employer designates the leave as FMLA leave, the leave taken does not count against an employee's FMLA entitlement.

(b) Nothing in this Act prevents an employer from amending existing leave and employee benefit programs, provided they comply with FMLA. However, nothing in the Act is intended to discourage employers from adopting o retaining more generous leave policies.

(c) The Act does not apply to employees under a collective bargaining agreement (CBA) in effect on August 5, 1993, until February 5, 1994, or the date the agreement terminates (*i.e.*, its expiration date), whichever is earlier. Thus, if the CBA contains family or medical leave benefits, whether greater or less than those under the Act, such benefits are not disturbed until the Act's provisions begin to apply to employees under that agreement. A CBA which provides no family or medical leave rights also continues in effect. For CBAs subject to the Railway Labor Act and other CBAs which do not have an expiration date for the general terms, but which may be reopened at specific times, *e.g.*, to amend wages and benefits, the first time the agreement is amended after August 5, 1993, shall be considered the termination date of the CBA, and the effective date for FMLA. It is contemplated that collective bargaining agreements will be amended to conform to FMLA during the extended effective date period.

§ 825.701 Do State laws providing family and medical leave still apply?

(a) Nothing in FMLA supersedes any provision of State or local law that provides greater family or medical leave rights than those provided by FMLA. The Department of Labor will not, however, enforce State family leave laws, and States may not enforce the FMLA. Employees are not required to designate whether the leave they are taking is FMLA leave or leave under State law, and an employer must comply with the appropriate (applicable) provisions of both. An employer covered by one law and not the other has to comply only with the law under which it is covered. Similarly, an employee eligible under only one law must receive benefits in accordance with that law. If leave qualifies for FMLA leave and leave under State law, the leave used counts against the employee's entitlement under both laws. Examples of the interaction between FMLA and State law include:

(1) If State law provides 16 weeks of leave entitlement over two years, an employee would be entitled to take 16 weeks one year under State law and 12 weeks the next year under FMLA. Health benefits maintenance under FMLA would be applicable only to the first 12 weeks of leave entitlement each year. If the employee took 12 weeks the first year, the employee would be entitled to a maximum of 12 weeks the second year under FMLA (not 16 weeks). An employee would not be entitled to 28 weeks in one year.

(2) If State law provides half-pay for employees temporarily disabled because of pregnancy for six weeks, the employee would be entitled to an additional six weeks of unpaid FMLA leave (or accrued paid leave).

(3) A shorter notice period under State law must be allowed by the employer unless an employer has already provided, or the employee is requesting, more leave than required under State law.

(4) If State law provides for only one medical certification, no additional certifications may be required by the employer unless the employer has already provided, or the employee is requesting, more leave than required under State law.

(5) If State law provides six weeks of leave, which may include leave to care for a seriously-ill grandparent or a "spouse equivalent," and leave was used for that purpose, the employee is still entitled to 12 weeks of FMLA leave, as the leave used was provided for a purpose not covered by FMLA. If FMLA leave is used first for a purpose also provided under State law, and State leave has thereby been exhausted, the employer would not be required to provide additional leave to care for the grandparent or "spouse equivalent."

(6) If State law prohibits mandatory leave beyond the actual period of pregnancy disability, an instructional employee of an educational agency subject to special FMLA rules may not be required to remain on leave until the end of the academic term, as permitted by FMLA under certain circumstances. (See Subpart F of this part.)

§ 825.702 How does FMLA affect Federal and State anti-discrimination laws?

(a) Nothing in FMLA modifies or affects any Federal or State law prohibiting discrimination on the basis of race, religion, color, national origin, sex, age, or disability. An employer must therefore comply with whichever statute provides the greater rights to employees. When an employer violates both FMLA and a discrimination law, an employee may be able to recover under either or both statutes.

(b) If an employee is a qualified individual with a disability within the meaning of the Americans with Disabilities Act (ADA), the employer must make reasonable accommodations, *etc.*, in accordance with the ADA. At the same time, the employer must afford an employee his or her FMLA rights. The examples in the following paragraphs of this section demonstrate how the two laws would interact with respect to a disabled employee.

(c) If an employee became disabled, a reasonable accommodation under the ADA might be accomplished by providing the employee with a part-time job with no health benefits. However, FMLA would permit an employee to work a reduced leave schedule until 12 weeks of leave were used, with health benefits maintained during this period. At the end of the FMLA leave entitlement, an employer is required to reinstate the employee in the same or an equivalent position, with equivalent pay and benefits, to that which the employee held when leave commenced. The employer's FMLA obligations would be satisfied if the employer offered the employee an equivalent full-time position. If the employee were unable to perform the equivalent position because of a disability, and the employee had exhausted his or her FMLA entitlement, the ADA may permit or require the employer to make a reasonable accommodation at that time by placing the employee in a part-time job, with only those benefits provided to part-time employees.

(d) If FMLA entitles an employee to leave, an employer may not, in lieu of FMLA leave entitlement, *require* an employee to take a job with a reasonable accommodation. However, ADA may require that an employer offer an employee the opportunity to take such a position.

(e) If an employer requires certifications of an employee's fitness for duty to return to work, as permitted by FMLA under a uniform policy, it must comply with the ADA requirement that a fitness for duty physical be job-related.

(f) For further information on Federal anti-discrimination laws, including the ADA, individuals are encouraged to contact the nearest office of the U.S. Equal Employment Opportunity Commission.

Subpart H—Definitions

§ 825.800 Definitions.

For purposes of this part:

Act or *FMLA* means the Family and Medical Leave Act of 1993, Public Law 103-3 (February 5, 1993), 107 Stat. 6 (29 U.S.C. 2601 *et seq.*)

Administrator means the Administrator of the Wage and Hour Division, Employment Standards Administration, U.S. Department of Labor, and includes any official of the Wage and Hour Division authorized to perform any of the functions of the Administrator under this part.

COBRA means the continuation coverage requirements of Title X of the Consolidated Omnibus Budget Reconciliation Act of 1986, As Amended (Pub.L. 99-272, title X, section 10002; 100 Stat 227; 29 U.S.C. 1161-1168).

Commerce and *industry or activity affecting commerce* mean any activity, business, or industry in commerce or in which a labor dispute would hinder or obstruct commerce or the free flow of commerce, and include "commerce" and any "industry affecting commerce" as defined in sections (501(1) and 501(3) of the Labor Management Relations Act of 1947, 29 U.S.C. 142(1) and (3).

Continuing treatment by a health care provider means one or more of the following:

(1) The employee or family member in question is treated two or more times for the injury or illness by a health care provider. Normally this would require visits to the health care provider or to a nurse or physician's assistant under direct supervision of the health care provider.

(2) The employee or family member is treated for the injury or illness two or more times by a provider of health care services (e.g., physical therapist) under orders of, or on referral by, a health care provider, *or* is treated for the injury or illness by a health care provider on at least one occasion which results in a regimen of continuing treatment under the supervision of the health care provider—for example, a course of medication or therapy—to resolve the health condition.

(3) The employee or family member is under the continuing supervision of, but not necessarily being actively treated by, a health care provider due to a serious long-term or chronic condition or disability which

cannot be cured. Examples include persons with Alzheimer's, persons who have suffered a severe stroke, or persons in the terminal states of a disease who may not be receiving active medical treatment.

Eligible employee means:

(1) An employee who has been employed for a total of at least 12 months by the employer on the date on which any FMLA leave is to commence; and

(2) Who, on the date on which any FMLA leave is to commence, has been employed for at least 1,250 hours of service with such employer during the previous 12-month period; and

(3) Excludes any Federal officer or employee covered under subchapter V of chapter 63 of title 5, United States Code; and

(4) Excludes any employee of the U.S. Senate or the U.S. House of Representatives covered under title V of the FMLA; and

(5) Excludes any employee who is employed at a worksite at which the employer employs fewer than 50 employees if the total number of employees employed by that employer within 75 miles of that worksite is also fewer than 50.

Employ means to suffer or permit to work.

Employee has the meaning given the same term as defined in section 3(e) of the Fair Labor Standards Act, 29 U.S.C. 203(e), as follows:

(1) The term "employee" means any individual employed by an employer;

(2) In case of an individual employed by a public agency, "employee: means—

(i) Any individual employed by the Government of the United States—

(A) As a civilian in the military departments (as defined in section 102 of Title 5, United States Code),

(B) In any executive agency (as defined in section 105 of Title 5, United States Code), excluding any Federal officer or employee covered under subchapter V of chapter 63 of Title 5, United States Code,

(C) In any unit of the legislative or judicial branch of the Government which has positions in the competitive service, excluding any employee of the U.S. Senate or U.S. House of Representatives who is covered under Title V of FMLA,

(D) In a nonappropriated fund instrumentality under the jurisdiction of the Armed Forces, or

(E) In the Library of Congress;

(ii) Any individual employed by the United States Postal Service or the Postal Rate Commission; and

(iii) Any individual employed by a State, political subdivision of a State, or an interstate governmental agency, other than such an individual—

(A) Who is not subject to the civil service laws of the State, political subdivision, or agency which employs the employee; and

(B) who—

(1) Holds a public elective office of that State, political subdivision, or agency,

(2) Is selected by the holder of such an office to be a member of his personal staff,

(3) Is appointed by such an officeholder to serve on a policymaking level,

(4) Is an immediate adviser to such an officeholder with respect to the constitutional or legal powers of the office of such officeholder, or

(5) Is an employee in the legislative branch or legislative body of that State, political subdivision, or agency and is not employed by the legislative library of such State, political subdivision, or agency.

Employee employed in an instructional capacity. See *Teacher*.

Employer means any person engaged in commerce or in an industry or activity affecting commerce who employs 50 or more employees for each working day during each of 20 or more calendar workweeks in the current or preceding calendar year, and includes—

(1) Any person who acts, directly or indirectly, in the interest of an employer to any of the employees of such employer;

(2) Any successor in interest of an employer; and

(3) Any public agency.

Employment benefits means all benefits provided or made available to employees by an employer, including group life insurance, health insurance, disability insurance, sick leave, annual leave, educational benefits, and pensions, regardless of whether such benefits are provided by a practice or written policy of an employer or though an "employee benefit plan" as defined in section 3(3) of the Employee Retirement Income Security Act of 1974, 29 U.S.C. 1002(3).

FLSA means the Fair Labor Standards Act (29 U.S.C. 201 *et seq.*).

Group health plan means any plan of, or contributed to by, an employer (including a self-insured plan) to provide health care (directly or otherwise) to the employer's employees, former employees, or the families of such employees or former employees.

Health care provider means:

(1) A doctor of medicine or osteopathy who is authorized to practice medicine or surgery by the State in which the doctor practices; or

(2) Podiatrists, dentists, clinical psychologists, optometrists, and chiropractors (limited to treatment consisting of manual manipulation of the spine to correct a subluxation as demonstrated by X-ray to exist) authorized to practice in the State and performing within the scope of their practice as defined under State law; and

(3) Nurse practitioners and nurse-midwives who are authorized to practice under State law and who are performing within the scope of their practice as defined under State law; and

(4) Christian Science practitioners listed with the First Church of Christ, Scientist in Boston, Massachusetts.

Incapable of self-care means that the individual requires active assistance or supervision to provide daily self-care in several of the "activities of daily living" or "ADLs." Activities of daily living include adaptive activities such as caring appropriately for one's grooming and hygiene, bathing, dressing, eating, cooking, cleaning, shopping, taking public transportation, paying bills, maintaining a residence, using telephones and directories, using a post office, etc.

Instructional employee: See *Teacher.*

Intermittent leave means leave taken in separate periods of time due to a single illness or injury, rather than for one continuous period of time, and may include leave of periods from an hour or more to several weeks. Examples of intermittent leave would include leave taken on an occasional basis for medical appointments, or leave taken several days at a time spread over a period of six months, such as for chemotherapy.

Mental disability: See *Physical or mental disability.*

Parent means the biological parent of an employee or an individual who stands or stood *in loco parentis* to an employee when the employee was a child. The term does *not* include parents "in law."

Person means an individual, partnership, association, corporation, business trust, legal representative, or any organized group of persons, and includes a public agency for purposes of this part.

Physical or mental disability means a physical or mental impairment that substantially limits one or more of the major life activities of an individual. Regulations at 29 CFR Part 1630, issued by the Equal Employment Opportunity Commission under the Americans with Disabilities Act (ADA), 42 U.S.C. 12101 *et seq.,* define these terms.

Public agency means the government of the United States; the government of a State or political subdivision thereof; any agency of the United States (including the United States Postal Service and Postal Rate Commission), a State or a political subdivision of a State, or any interstate governmental agency. Under section 101(5)(B) of the Act, a public agency is considered to be a "person" engaged in commerce or in an industry or activity affecting commerce within the meaning of the Act.

Reduced leave schedule means a leave schedule that reduces the usual number of hours per workweek, or hours per workday, of an employee.

Secretary means the Secretary of Labor or authorized representatives.

Serious health condition means an illness, injury, impairment, or physical or mental condition that involves:

(1) Any period of incapacity or treatment in connection with or consequent to inpatient care (*i.e.,* an overnight stay) in a hospital, hospice, or residential medical care facility;

(2) Any period of incapacity requiring absence from work, school, or other regular daily activities, of more than three calendar days, that also involves continuing treatment by (or under the supervision of) a health care provider; or

(3) Continuing treatment by (or under the supervision of) a health care provider for a chronic or long-term health condition that is incurable or so serious that, if not treated, would likely result in a period of incapacity of more than three calendar days; and for prenatal care.

(4) Voluntary or cosmetic treatments (such as most treatments for orthodontia or acne) which are not medically necessary are not "serious health conditions," unless inpatient hospital care is required. Restorative dental surgery after an accident, or removal of cancerous growths are serious health conditions provided all the other conditions of this regulation are met. Treatments for allergies or stress, or for substance abuse, are serious health conditions if all the conditions of the regulation are met. Prenatal care is included as a serious health condition. Routine preventive physical examinations are excluded.

Son or daughter means a biological, adopted, or foster child, a stepchild, a legal ward, or a child of a person standing *in loco parentis,* who is under 18 years of age *or* 18 years of age or older an incapable of self-care because of a mental or physical disability.

Spouse means a husband or wife as defined or recognized under State law for purposes of marriage, including common law marriage in States where it is recognized.

State means any State of the United States or the District of Columbia or any Territory or possession of the United States.

Teacher (or *employee employed in an instructional capacity,* or *instructional employee*) means an employee employed principally in an instructional capacity by an educational agency or school whose principal function is to reach and instruct students in a class, a small group, or an individual setting, and includes athletic coaches, driving instructors, and special education assistants such as signers for the hearing impaired. The term does not include teacher assistants or aides who do not have as their principal function actual teaching or instructing, nor auxiliary personnel such as counselors, psychologists, curriculum specialists, cafeteria workers, maintenance workers, bus drivers, or other primarily noninstructional employees.

APPENDIX A to PART 825–INDEX

The citations listed in this Appendix are to sections in 29 CFR Part 825.

Appendix B to Part 825—Certification of Physician or Practitioner

Appendix C to Part 825—Notice to Employees of Rights under FMLA

APPENDIXES

A. Model Family and Medical Leave Policy

B. Sample FMLA Notice to Employees

C. DOL Form for Certification of Physician or Practitioner

APPENDIX A

MODEL FAMILY AND MEDICAL LEAVE POLICY

[WARN] This sample policy does not constitute legal advice. The policy should not be used without being modified to accomodate both the requirements of state law and the needs of individual employers.

MODEL
FAMILY AND MEDICAL LEAVE POLICY

I. DEFINITIONS

A. FAMILY AND MEDICAL CARE LEAVE

Leave taken for the care of a son or daughter, spouse, or parent who has a serious health condition.

B. PREGNANCY DISABILITY LEAVE

Leave taken because of personal medical disability due to pregnancy or childbirth. Employees should first use their rights to leave under the company Pregnancy Disability Leave policy. If additional leave is needed, they may apply for Personal Illness Leave under this policy.

C. CHILDCARE LEAVE

Within one year of the birth of a son or daughter, or of placement with an employee of a son or daughter for adoption or foster care, the employee may request a leave for childcare.

D. PERSONAL ILLNESS LEAVE

Leave for personal illness due to serious health conditions. Employees may also be eligible under the company Sick Leave Policy and under the company Disability Policy for leaves for personal illness.

E. MATERNITY LEAVE

A general term for a leave or combination of leaves taken under pregnancy disability, childcare, family care and medical or personal illness leaves of absence.

II. ELIGIBLE EMPLOYEES

A. Employees who have been employed for at least 12 months and who have worked at least 1,250 hours during the last twelve months.

III. LENGTH OF LEAVES

A. Employees may take up to a total of 12 weeks of unpaid leave every 12 months. The 12-month period is calculated backwards from the starting date of the requested leave. Employees must return when the conditions of the leave no longer exist. Failure to return or to be approved for another type of company leave will result in termination.

B. Leaves may be taken on an intermittent basis when medically necessary. The need for intermittent leaves for serious health conditions must be supported by medical certification. Employees taking intermittent leaves may be temporarily transferred to equivalent positions.

C. The minimum period for childcare leaves is generally two weeks. The minimum leave period for family and personal medical care leaves is one hour.

IV. SUBSTITUTION/DESIGNATION OF LEAVES

A. Employees with serious health conditions who apply for vacation, personal leave, sick leave, or disability leave will have such time designated by the company as Family and Medical Care Leave. Employees who apply for vacation or personal leave for childcare will have such time designated by the company as Family and Medical Care Leave. (This means that Family and Medical Care Leaves may run simultaneously with other approved leaves.)

B. Employees who take approved company leaves may, if qualified, substitute such leaves for Family and Medical Care Leaves.

C. Employees who are disabled due to pregnancy or childbirth related conditions may take a Pregnancy Disability Leave and, if needed, the full 12 weeks of Family and Medical Care Leave.

V. CERTIFICATION

A. Request for leave of absence for serious health conditions of the employee or family member must include a health care provider certification. Employees may request a health care provider certification form from the Human Resources Department. The company may require an examination by a company selected health care provider if the leave is due to a serious health condition of the employee.

B. Employees returning from a personal illness leave will be required to obtain a health care provider's certification that the employee is able to return to work and can perform the essential functions of his/her job. Employees may not start work without providing such certification to the Human Resources Department.

VI. PAY DURING LEAVE

A. Leaves taken under this policy are without pay except that salaried/ exempt employees will be paid for family and personal medical care leaves of less than one day.

VII. MEDICAL AND OTHER PAID BENEFITS

A. Health care coverage. Employee health care coverage will continue during family care leaves. Employees are responsible for the employee paid portion of the premiums. Failure to pay the employee paid portion of the premiums will result in lapse of coverage.

B. Other Employee Benefit Plans. Employees may continue other benefit plans as permitted by the plan including pension, 401(k), life, disability, etc. by arranging for advance payroll deductions or by making the appropriate payments to the Human Resources Department.

VIII. JOB RESTORATION

A. Employees will return from Family and Medical Leaves to their same or equivalent positions. In the event of elimination of the position, the employee will be returned to a comparable position.

B. Highly Compensated Employees. Certain highly compensated employees may be notified before or during their leaves that their position cannot be held open. If these employees take or continue the leave, they are not guaranteed any position upon return.

IX. ADVANCE NOTIFICATION

A. Employees who anticipate taking a Family or Medical Leave are required to fill out an application for Family or Medical Leave and to submit it to the Human Resources Department with medical certification, if appropriate, at least thirty (30) days in advance of the leave. Failure to request a leave, where such leave was anticipated, is grounds for denial of the leave.

APPENDIX B

SAMPLE FMLA NOTICE TO EMPLOYEES

[WARN] The following is a sample notice that covered employers are required to post regarding rights and responsibilities under the FMLA. This notice was issued in June 1993.[1] Prior to posting any notice, the employer should contact the Department of Labor at (202) 219-8412 to obtain the most recent version.

YOUR RIGHTS
under the
FAMILY AND MEDICAL LEAVE ACT OF 1993

FMLA requires covered employers to provide up to 12 weeks of unpaid, job-protected leave to "eligible" employees for certain family and medical reasons. Employees are eligible if they have worked for a covered employer for at least one year, and for 1,250 hours over the previous 12 months, and if there are at least 50 employees within 75 miles.

REASONS FOR TAKING LEAVE: Unpaid leave must be granted for *any* of the following reasons:

- to care for the employee's child after birth, or placement for adoption or foster care;
- to care for the employee's spouse, son or daughter, or parent, who has a serious health condition; or
- for a serious health condition that makes the employee unable to perform the employee's job.

At the employee's or employer's option, certain kinds of *paid* leave may be substituted for unpaid leave.

[1] Daily Labor Report (BNA), June 4, 1993.

ADVANCE NOTICE AND MEDICAL CERTIFICATION: The employee may be required to provide advance leave notice and medical certification. Taking of leave may be denied if requirements are not met.

- The employee ordinarily must provide 30 days advance notice when the leave is "foreseeable."
- An employer may require medical certification to support a request for leave because of a serious health condition, and may require second or third opinions (at the employer's expense) and a fitness for duty report to return to work.

JOB BENEFITS AND PROTECTION:

- For the duration of FMLA leave, the employer must maintain the employee's health coverage under any "group health plan."
- Upon return from FMLA leave, most employees must be restored to their original or equivalent positions with equivalent pay, benefits, and other employment terms.
- The use of FMLA leave cannot result in the loss of any employment benefit that accrued prior to the start of an employee's leave.

UNLAWFUL ACTS BY EMPLOYERS: FMLA makes it unlawful for any employer to:

- interfere with, restrain, or deny the exercise of any right provided under FMLA;
- discharge or discriminate against any person for opposing any practice made unlawful by FMLA or for involvement in any proceeding under or relating to FMLA.

ENFORCEMENT:

- The U.S. Department of Labor is authorized to investigate and resolve complaints of violations.
- An eligible employee may bring a civil action against an employer for violations.

FMLA does not affect any federal or state law prohibiting discrimination, or supersede any state or local law or collective bargaining agreement which provides greater family or medical leave rights.

<u>FOR ADDITIONAL INFORMATION:</u> Contact the nearest office of the Wage and Hour Division, listed in most telephone directories under U.S. Government, Department of Labor.

U.S. Department of Labor, Employment Standards Administration
WH Publication 1420
Wage and Hour Division, Washington, D.C. 20210 June 1993

APPENDIX C

DOL FORM FOR CERTIFICATION OF PHYSICIAN OR PRACTITIONER

The following is the Department of Labor (DOL) certification form to support certain leave requests. This form is not required; other wording that meets the requirements of the FMLA is acceptable. For questions concerning this form and other FMLA issues related to the DOL, contact the Department of Labor at (202) 219–8412.

DOL FORM FOR CERTIFICATION OF PHYSICIAN OR PRACTITIONER

U.S. Department of Labor
Employment Standards Administration
Wage and Hour Division

CERTIFICATION OF PHYSICIAN OR PRACTITIONER
(Family and Medical Leave Act of 1993)

1. Employee's Name:

2. Patient's Name (If other than employee):

3. Diagnosis:

4. Date condition commenced:

5. Probable duration of condition:

6. Regimen of treatment to be prescribed (Indicate number of visits, general nature and duration of treatment, including referral to other provider of health services. Include schedule of visits or treatment if it is medically necessary for the employee to be off work on an intermittent basis or to work less than the employee's normal schedule of hours per day or days per week.):

   a. By Physician or Practitioner:

   b. By another provider of health services, if referred by Physician or Practitioner:

IF THIS CERTIFICATION RELATES TO CARE FOR THE EMPLOYEE'S SERIOUSLY-ILL FAMILY MEMBER, SKIP ITEMS 7, 8 AND 9 AND PROCEED TO ITEMS 10 THRU 14 ON REVERSE SIDE. OTHERWISE, CONTINUE BELOW.

Check Yes or No in the boxes below, as appropriate.

	Yes	No	
7.	☐	☐	Is inpatient hospitalization of the employee required?
8.	☐	☐	Is employee able to perform work of any kind? (If "No," skip Item 9.)
9.	☐	☐	Is employee able to perform the functions of employee's position? (Answer after reviewing statement from employer of essential functions of employee's position, or, if none provided, after discussing with employee.)

15. Signature of Physician or Practitioner:

16. Date:

17. Type of Practice (Field of Specialization, if any):

FOR CERTIFICATION RELATING TO CARE FOR THE EMPLOYEE'S SERIOUSLY-ILL FAMILY MEMBER, COMPLETE ITEMS 10 THRU 14 BELOW AS THEY APPLY TO THE FAMILY MEMBER AND PROCEED TO ITEM 15 ON REVERSE SIDE.

	Yes	No	
10.	☐	☐	Is inpatient hospitalization of the family member (patient) required?
11.	☐	☐	Does (or will) the patient require assistance for basic medical, hygiene, nutritional needs, safety or transportation?
12.	☐	☐	After review of the employee's signed statement (*See* Item 14 below), is the employee's presence necessary or would it be beneficial for the care of the patient? (This may include psychological comfort.)

13. Estimate the period of time care is needed or the employee's presence would be beneficial:

ITEM 14 IS TO BE COMPLETED BY THE EMPLOYEE NEEDING FAMILY LEAVE.

14. When Family Leave is needed to care for a seriously-ill family member, the employee shall state the care he or she will provide and an estimate of the time period during which this care will be provided, including a schedule if leave is to be taken intermittently or on a reduced leave schedule:

Employee signature:

Date:

INDEX